What the f?

The Photographic Adventures of Erica Lane Harvey
51 Photo Stories with *Tips!* from What She Learned Along the Way

---

Stories, Tips & Photography by Erica Lane Harvey
Writing, Layout & Design by Antonia Marie Kucera
(It's a little bit of both of us on pretty much everything!)

This book is proudly made in the USA

Self-published by Erica Lane Photography, LLC
Produced at Bang Printing in Minnesota
Library of Congress Control Number: 2020922607 • ISBN: 978-0-578-75575-5

Copyright ® 2021 by Erica Lane Photography. All rights reserved. No part of this publication may be reproduced, stored in a retrieval system, or transmitted in any form or by any means – electronic, mechanical, audio recording, or otherwise – without the written permission of the self-publishing party, Erica Lane Photography, LLC, except in the case of reviews and certain other noncommercial uses permitted by copyright law. Please contact Erica Lane Photography with requests, contact information can be found at www.EricaLanePhotography.com. Any product names, logos, brands or trademarks featured or referred to in this publication are the property of their respective trademark owners. Names in stories are used with the respective person's permission.

Portrait by Edgar Matuska

DEDICATION with love

To My Parents, Mary Beth and Charlie Johnson

This book is dedicated, with much love, to my parents. Thank you for teaching me joy in life, such as laughing at my goofy face when reviewing the family portrait proofs! (Yep, that's me in the middle, winking!)

It is not easy for a parent when their child decides they want to grow up to be an artist... oh, and let's not forget also wanting to be a race car driver! (Third graders have DREAMS, you know.) I wasn't the easy-going kid who set my parent's mind at ease by wanting to be a lawyer or doctor, professions that usually mean security in life.

It's more likely assumed that life as an artist will be a struggle, and success is definitely not guaranteed… and yet, not once do I remember my parents saying, "Don't do that." If anything, they've constantly stood behind me, pushing me and encouraging me to be the best I could be, to always believe in myself.

When I look back at my earlier work, I marvel that they didn't tell me to give up. My work wasn't award winning then, yet they supported me as I kept trying… and trying… and trying. Life as a photographer – especially one who gallivants about, more often capturing sunsets instead of wedding ceremonies – means a reliable income is uncertain, and parents just want their children to be safe and secure. Still, my parents continually encouraged me to chase my dreams. I'm not sure many parents would do such a thing in the face of uncertainty, and I will be forever grateful that my parents took the chance.

This book and the work therein would not be here today without their belief in me and what I could accomplish.

Mom, Dad, I love you both with all my heart and I hope I make you proud.

Photo by Antonia Kucera

GOOD TO KNOW
what the *f* is with that title

The Title, Explained... Only Half As Vulgar As You May Think!

I'm hoping the title of this book made you laugh, but I wanted to take a minute to explain the double meaning behind my first ever photo book, **"What the f?"**

My fellow photographers already know the first meaning, but for those who are just here for the pretty pictures, I'll let you in on the meaning. **The letter "*f*" – especially when italicized in a serif font - is used to denote the aperture setting in the photography world.** I'm sure if you've ever heard a group of photographers geek out on their passion, you've realized we have our own lingo! The aperture itself is created by a layer of overlapping flaps inside the lens, and it can widen and close like the iris of your eye to control the amount of light coming into your camera. If you could look inside a lens and see the aperture, it looks a bit like the symbol that creates the bottom half of the question mark on the cover of the book! Like this: ❂ (You'll see this little symbol throughout the book at the end of each story.)

The second meaning behind the title encompasses the subject matter of this book. You see, this is more than a photography book. Have you ever looked at a great photo and wondered if there was a story behind it? There usually is, and that's the purpose behind every image chosen for this book. There's a story behind each photo, and not just regular stories – each story has an instance that made me go "What the f?!?!" (or something like it) in my head.

"What the f?" can encompass so many emotions and experiences. They can be moments of joyful surprise, or moments of trepidation, fear, shock, humor or disappointment.

I wanted to share these moments, these stories, in the hopes that you'll enjoy my adventures and misadventures as much as I have. Maybe you'll relate to some stories, or maybe you'll just think I'm a bit crazy. I hope, at the very least, that you love the photos.

Now, let's go take in a fresh breath of mountain air!

in the book - contents

Let the Adventure Begin – THE START

DEDICATION, WITH LOVE 3
To my parents, Mary Beth and Charlie Johnson

GOOD TO KNOW 5
The Title Explained... Only Half As Vulgar As You May Think

FOREWORD 13
By Johnny Sundby

ABOUT ERICA 14
Photographer | Adventurer | Dog Mom | Art Lover | Nature Enthusiast

Time to Explore – THE STORIES

SOMETHING TO APPRECIATE 22
Morro Rock State Preserve | California, United States

THE MOST WHAT THE F? STORY EVER 24
Bighorn Mountains | Wyoming, United States

THE TRIP THAT STARTED MY OBSESSION 31
Santorini, Greece

BETTER THAN DREAMING IN BED 32
Devils Tower National Monument | Wyoming, United States

WHEN IN DOUBT, GET UP AND GO 35
Glacier National Park | Montana, United States

THE SADNESS BEHIND THE BEAUTY 36
Mosi-oa-Tunya National Park | Zambia, Africa

PUSHING BOUNDARIES 39
Mosi-oa-Tunya National Park | Zambia, Africa

A BIG SURPRISE 40
Yellowstone National Park | Wyoming, United States

A GLOOMY AND GRIZZLY EXPERIENCE 42
Grand Teton National Park | Wyoming, United States

YEAH, SURE, COWS... 44
Grand Teton National Park | Wyoming, United States

FRIENDS KEEP US MOTIVATED 46
Banff National Park | Alberta, Canada

HOW TO PISS OFF TOURISTS 50
Banff National Park | Alberta, Canada

NO TIME FOR INSURANCE 52
Jasper National Park | Alberta, Canada

SUNRISE WITH PRESIDENTS AND STRANGERS 54
Mount Rushmore National Memorial | The Black Hills, South Dakota

MY MOM'S ALL-TIME FAVORITE STORY 56
Grand Teton National Park | Wyoming, United States

1996

2008

AREN'T PARKS SUPPOSED TO BE PEACEFUL? 58
Grand Teton National Park | Wyoming, United States

WELL THAT WAS UNEXPECTED 60
Grand Teton National Park | Wyoming, United States

GEYSERS AREN'T AFRAID OF THE DARK. 63
Yellowstone National Park | Wyoming, United States

TEMPERAMENTAL ICE 66
Spearfish Canyon, The Black Hills | South Dakota, United States

ODDLY SATISFYING 71
Custer State Park | South Dakota, United States

ALWAYS DOUBLE CHECK. 73
Pactola Reservoir in the Black Hills | South Dakota, United States

PLEASE DON'T GORE ME.... 75
Glacier National Park | Montana, United States

THE UN-HEARTBREAK HOTEL 76
Banff National Park | Alberta, Canada

SPUR OF THE MOMENT 80
Jasper National Park | Alberta, Canada

EXPLORE, SNOOZE, REPEAT 82
Glacier National Park | Montana, United States

BISON JAMS AND FINDING GOLD 84
Yellowstone National Park | Wyoming, United States

SO THAT'S WHAT FROSTBITE FEELS LIKE.... 86
Badlands National Park | South Dakota, United States

CRAP, WHICH ROAD WAS IT? 88
Bear Butte | South Dakota, United States

WHAT THE FOX IS GOING ON? 90
Yellowstone National Park | Wyoming, United States

THEY HAVE WHAT NOW?!?!........................ 92
Badlands National Park | South Dakota, United States

THE BUNNY WHO SAVED ME 95
Wind Cave National Park | South Dakota, United States

TAKE THE RISK, OR NOT? 96
Grand Teton National Park | Wyoming, United States

IN FOR A TREAT 99
Grand Teton National Park | Wyoming, United States

DAY OF DISCOVERY 100
Custer State Park | South Dakota, United States

WE'RE GOING ON AN ADVENTURE! 102
Franz Josef Glacier | Westland Tai Poutini National Park | South Island, New Zealand

GLAD WE BOUGHT INSURANCE... 107
Milford Sound | South Island, New Zealand

BEAR-LY HOLDING ON 108
Grand Teton National Park | Wyoming, United States

A TOTALITY EPIC ADVENTURE..................... 110
Total Solar Eclipse | Somewhere near the Wyoming border, United States

HOW DID I MISS THAT?	115
Banff National Park | Alberta, Canada	
BACK AND FORTH, BACK AND FORTH	118
Banff National Park | Alberta, Canada	
SOMETIMES THINGS GO SIDEWAYS	120
Port Campbell National Park | The Great Ocean Road, Australia	
WORTH EVERY PENNY	122
Uluru-Kata Tjuta National Park | Northern Territory, Australia	
THIS IS NOT A HAPPY PICTURE	124
Kakadu National Park | Darwin, Australia	
THE PHOTO THAT COST A FORTUNE	126
Royal Botanical Gardens in Sydney | New South Wales, Australia	
THE BADGER BABES	128
Grand Teton National Park | Wyoming, United States	
WORTH THE COST?	131
Lake Clark National Park | Alaska, United States	
DINNER IS SERVED	134
Protected Waters of Annette Island | Alaska, United States	
EXPECT THE UNEXPECTED	136
Custer State Park | South Dakota, United States	
DON'T WAIT FOR RETIREMENT	138
Northern Rocky Mountains | Colorado, United States	
TAKING ANOTHER LOOK	141
Bear Butte Area | South Dakota, United States	
BONUS: 2020 WAS A BLAST, RIGHT?!?!	142
Mount Rushmore National Memorial | South Dakota, United States	

Erica's Top 5/Top 5 - THE TIPS

THE CAMERAS	152
QUALITY GEAR	154
SHOOTING TIPS	160
DIGITAL EDITING	166
WILDLIFE SPOTS	172
FAVORITE LOCATIONS	182
BONUS TIP: ORGANIZATIONS	192

Make Every Day An Adventure - THE END

FINAL WORD	196
Best Friends and Travel Buddies, Decades in the Making | By Antonia Kucera	
THANK YOU	198
With Gratitude To Our Kickstarter Backers & Other Supporters	
IN LOVING MEMORY	200
Thanks for All the Cuddles, Wiggles and Giggles	

"Life is about collecting memories, not things."

LET THE
adventure
BEGIN

Travel with me through the adventure of life, as I discover a passion for photography and explore this beautiful place we call Earth.

SPECIAL THANKS TO:

ALT Illustration's Alyssa Tanner for illustrating our fun stickers!
Johnny Sundby for editing and the lovely foreword. :)
Russell Jensen for editing the tips section.
Richard Kucera for editing and other dad wisdom.
Georgene Parker for the final round of editing.
Michael Linn at Linn Productions for creating our Kickstarter videos!
Gator Grip's Tracy Malioux for awesome B-Roll.

Nothing Like Mom's Homemade Clam Chowder Image Composite | First Place, Landscape/Nature Category, PPA's 2020 Grand Imaging Awards   July 2018

ERICA LANE
PHOTOGRAPHY LLC

www.EricaLanePhotography.com | Rapid City, South Dakota

foreword

M. Photog. Cr., CPP | Johnny Sundby Photography Inc.

I've been honored to help edit this book, and I was shocked at how much I enjoyed that task! It's an inspirational, gorgeous book filled with even-more amazing photos, plus beautifully written, personal stories that will have you laughing, crying, and saying "Amen" right out loud!

I've spent nearly my entire life in photography, with more than 30 years as a professional, but a few years ago, I was fortunate enough to meet a young woman leading the Black Hills Photography Club by the name of Erica Lane Harvey. I was struck by her professionalism as she led the meeting, and by her leadership and intelligence, but most especially by the images that she presented in a photo contest I judged.

In the parking lot, we visited more, and I asked if she'd help out at my studio. Our professional relationship grew. We taught classes together to aspiring and professional photographers alike via the Professional Photographers of America (PPA). We made images together and attended photography conventions and workshops. I have learned a great deal from Erica, including much about landscape composition, equipment (mine's basically all old), and post-processing. She has reminded me of my own love of photography that sometimes wanes in the daily grind of running a studio year after year.

She rose like a rock star in the PPA, winning awards for her prints, including two Grand Imaging entries (top ten in the USA) – where "Nothing Like Mom's Homemade Clam Chowder" (at left) won first prize. She earned her Master of Photography in a record three years (it took me 10), Master Craftsman in the same amount of time, plus Certified Professional Photographer. All of these are major PPA milestones that few professional photographers achieve.

We visited often, and still visit often, about this and that as it relates to photography. She is only a phone call away when our studio needs some help, although usually she is already committed to her own endeavors!

Erica has a bachelor's degree in photography from Brooks Institute of Photography, plus a master's degree from the University of South Dakota in Administrative Studies. Her work ethic, superior people skills, absolute love of photography, and her attention to detail make her images magical and capture the attention of some of the nation's best photographers.

It's been a pleasure calling Erica my friend these past few years, and I publicly thank her for her contribution to the art (which I like to call vocation) of photography.

Enjoy! *Johnny Sundby*

ABOUT ERICA
who the *f* is this chick?

Photographer | Adventurer | Dog Mom | Art Lover | Nature Enthusiast

---

I've had my fair share of "What the *f?*" moments in my life! Some are good, some are sad, but these moments make us who we are. They add up to create a lifetime of experiences that drive us and fuel our passions. They shaped me.

As a result of growing up in the Black Hills, one of my main passions is caring for the world around us, and protecting all the beautiful nature that is essential for life. Photography, it just so happens, is the perfect tool to share this with you! Plus I like art and all things pretty, cute or fluffy, like my teacup poodle, Peanut.

DISCOVERING PHOTOGRAPHY

Photography was a natural fit for me. My mom actually figured this out through an early "What the...?" moment in my life! I was just eight years old when mom took a local photography class and brought home that snazzy, shiny, cool looking camera. I couldn't wait to get my hands on it! I was a curious and rambunctious kid and that camera drew me like a moth to a flame.

Mom let me "play" with it, but only under supervision – it was a Canon AE-1 Program, which was a professional level camera at that time. Not a toy! I loved taking pictures with it. I'd mess with the settings, shoot pics out in the woods... then I'd have to wait for developed film to figure out what all those settings had done! I even won a photo contest that year with a picture I took of a deer in the Black Hills. It just came naturally to me and I figured it out with no instruction.

By the end of the photography class, mom had her fill of photography but seemed to know that I was just getting started. I'm guessing she had a WTF moment when she realized her eight-year-old understood the camera better than she did! She gladly gave me the camera, saying, "I think you're supposed to have this."

▲ The bandana days (long hair gets in the way) with my first ever real camera, the Canon AE-1 Program

And that camera stuck with me all the way through high school. I continued taking pictures as a hobby and took classes at school for fun. I loved it more and more and then thought, well heck… I may as well make a living doing what I love! Young and full of vim and vigor, I headed to California in 1999 to go to one of the best photography schools in the world, Brooks Institute of Photography in sunny Santa Barbara, and I finally bought my first Nikon, the N90s.

Let's take a sec to explain a little something about the photography world: Canon vs. Nikon is a bit like PC vs. Mac in the computer world. The cameras work a bit differently – especially with the "user interface" if we stick with the computer analogy – and the users of each brand are pretty loyal. Both brands can take amazing pictures, of course, but picking a brand can be a lifetime investment. Once you get used to your camera and get a couple of lenses, you don't usually want to switch. (A Nikon lens won't fit a Canon, and vice versa.)

In all honesty, the only reason I chose Nikon at first was because I couldn't reach the newer Canon buttons with my poor thumb! At the time, Canons apparently were not built for petite gals. I've never looked back though – I love my Nikon gear! (See? Loyal fan!)

All right, back to my life and why the *f* I'm me…

▲ Traveling superstars Everett Preston (know as Ep) and Grace Howe, my awesome grandparents

DISCOVERING MYSELF

I was excited for college – to dive into the more technical study, to play with artistic angles, and to see how others have made careers out of photography. I always loved working in the darkroom, so I chose color film printing as my major, or "focus" as they called it at Brooks. A note for the digital era readers – color film was much more technical and tougher to print than B&W film, so yes, it was a full course of study at the school!

But life decided to throw me a curve ball. I took a sabbatical from school for medical reasons in my middle year, and when I returned they had dropped my focus! What the *f!* I could no longer study color film processing because – you guessed it – digital was taking over. Uggghhhh! I was resistant to digital at this point because, in my (ahem, rightful) opinion, the quality was nowhere near film. I mean, seriously, my first camera had 6 megapixels!!! (Now I have 45 MP.)

I had to choose something though, so I switched to journalism with the youthful ideal of helping people and saving the world! (OK, I still try to do that… hey, it's a good ideal to have!) I finished school and graduated in 2003.

I'd planned on staying in California after school, but something much more important brought me home. My beloved grandfather's health was failing, and I rushed back to spend as much time with him as I could. My grandfather, Everett Preston or "Ep" Howe, and my grandmother Grace, who had passed away a few years before, were a big influence on another passion that drives my photography – TRAVEL! What better way to appreciate the world around us than to go out and see it? I have a world map on my

The mysterious Erica Lane Harvey in her natural habitat ▲

wall that my grandparents had kept with pins marking all the places they'd visited in the world. Next to it now is my own map that I've started with pins marking the places I've traveled to. I've still got a lot of the world to see!

But this brings us to a sad WTF moment in my life – my grandfather did pass away, and our whole family took it hard. We still miss him, but it's wonderful what an inspiration he and my grandmother were to the next generations of our family. I think we're all doing them proud.

I decided to stay in Rapid City to start my own photography career, but that was easier said than done, ha! I came upon a whole series of WTF moments at this point in my life.

For one thing, photography businesses in the area had blown up. Where there had only been a few portrait photographers in the area when I'd left for school, now there seemed to be one on every corner! Also, the local newspaper wasn't hiring, and when I even offered to work for FREE, their current editors ~politely~ declined, saying they had more than enough photographers. My now-friend and peer Johnny Sundby, who wrote the foreword for this book and worked at the newspaper back in the day, was surprised when I told him this story years later! He was aware of my journalism degree and just couldn't believe the paper hadn't taken me up on my offer!

At one point a friend told me of a job at a local ad agency. I ended up getting hired for commercial work, including shooting and editing video, which I'd only ever had two classes in! I was up for the challenge, of course, eager at any opportunity to apply my skills and learn more through experience. But the grunt work just didn't feed the artist in me, I needed more creative freedom! I decided to take the plunge and started my own business in 2005.

One of the things 2020 taught me is to fully appreciate things normally taken for granted, like the value of small businesses in our communities. Seeing people lose their livelihoods is heartbreaking, especially if it's a business that they've built up from bare bones, work that takes YEARS. When I started my business back in 2005, I had no idea what I was getting myself into, and how long it would take to build things up! But I was doing it. I'd secured a gallery and studio spot downtown, and business – from weddings and portraits to commercial work – started to come my way.

Then 2008 came, and the economy took a nosedive. WTF? My business went with it.

But hey, I'm adaptable! I actually did a 180 and surprised everyone in my life by GIVING UP photography!!! I actually decided to go back to school, NOT for photography, this time taking online classes from 2009-2011; I earned a

▼ *Maybe the economy is somewhere up there???*

business degree, graduating with a 4.0 – something my high school self would have been shocked by! That was an excited-woo-hoo WTF moment!

I went on a tour of Asia in 2011 to celebrate my accomplishment, and I didn't even take a hobbyist level camera with me, much less a professional one. Weird, I know! I worked at a framing shop and art gallery around this time, and even had the opportunity to buy the business (it wasn't a good fit for me at the time). So my Asia trip fed my other passion, traveling, and I felt content getting exposure to art at the gallery... but I was starting to miss photography.

DISCOVERING LOVE

It was at this time in my life that I met my husband. Adam had first noticed me in a martial arts class we both attended, and oddly, he started seeing me pop up everywhere. He noticed me once at a young professionals gathering – he's in the mailing business – and even remembered me being at his work place from my ad agency years. After seeing me at a mutual friend's wedding, he called up the bride and said, "Hey, you got any single friends who would be interested in a tall guy with dancer's legs?" (I'm not joking, I'm quoting her!)

Our mutual friend knew that I had just come out of a bad breakup, coincidentally with a guy from the martial arts class. But she didn't know that just before she called me about Adam, I had literally sworn off dating for a while! I couldn't think if I knew this guy she wanted to set me up with, but I trusted her judgement and thought, "Well, it's just dinner..." so I said yes.

After an hour of overthinking, I second guessed myself... what the *f* was I thinking? I had just sworn off dating! At this point I thought to ask her for a picture of the mystery guy, wondering if I knew him. She sent the most awkward, god-awful cell phone pic that Adam still can't believe she sent me. Ha! I recognized him from the martial arts academy, which reminded me again of my recent breakup and that I was in the middle of second guessing my decision to date...

▲ Lovebirds in the mountains!

Despite the awkward photo and overthinking my decision, I stuck to my commitment. And I'm sooooooo glad I took a chance! We hit it off and started dating officially, falling for each other quickly.

Adam first discovered my passion for travel when he shared with me that his family had taken a cruise together and he'd loved going on that trip. Much to his surprise, I showed up to our next date with cruise brochures so we could plan a trip! This was three months into our relationship. Thankfully Adam didn't see it as a red flag!

We continued to date, travel, and fall in love, and in August of 2011 on a trip to Yellowstone, Adam proposed.

Funny side story here... my mom has an accidental habit of ruining Adam's surprises for me. Before our Yellowstone trip, my mom had called me to ask what time we were coming for dinner. I replied, "Uh... we're not, I'm hanging out with a friend tonight." My mom was confused and said something about Adam having called... I suddenly realized what the only reason would be for Adam to go ALONE to my parent's house, and in a panic said to my mom, "We have to stop talking!!!" then I hung up on her!

But even if that hadn't happened, I still would have accidentally ruined the surprise of Adam's proposal on the trip itself. Early on in the trip I was making some tea while Adam showered after a long hike. While digging through his bag looking for sugar, I stumbled onto the ring box. Oops!

So when he got down on one knee by Yellowstone Lake and popped the question, I did my best to make a surprise face. Apparently my acting skills suck, because poor Adam was staring at me with a funny look, waiting for me to answer. So he said, "Well?!?" and I finally remembered to reply. "OH... yes!!!"

Later that night I told him about how I'd already found the ring box, to explain my pause. Since that was enough of a

shock, I waited five years before telling him my mom had already accidentally ruined the surprise!

After we married and moved in together with our little dogs (my teacup poodle Peanut and his papillon Dizzy), I was happy in love and happy with our travels... but something was missing for me. Just seeing and enjoying the beauty in the world wasn't enough. I wanted to capture it and share it. I missed photography with all of my heart and soul.

DISCOVERING PASSION

At this time, I managed to give Adam an even bigger shock than the revelation of the travel addiction. After deciding not to buy the frame shop, my framing career came to an end when they couldn't afford to keep me on anymore. Since I missed photography so much, I thought this was the perfect time to take it up again. I told Adam out of the blue that I wanted to go into business for myself doing photography. I don't think he believed me!!!

I was actually expecting a really big WTF-type reaction here, but didn't get it. Remember, he'd met me when I'd given up photography. He had absolutely NO idea what I could do with a camera, and how driven I could be once I start taking photos. But he was incredibly supportive regardless – he said as long as we could pay the bills, I could take on my dream. (Thanks, honey!)

I took on my profession with a new fervor this time. I studied and researched about all the advancements in digital photography. I took off for sunrise and sunset shoots whenever possible to hone my skills after six years of sparse use. I joined a business networking group (BNI), plus a specialized master level organization, Professional Photographers of America (PPA). I've learned so much more this time around! Heck, I looked back at my younger self and wasn't surprised I hadn't made it – I just hadn't possessed the knowledge or support to survive an economic downturn.

By now, life's many experiences have taught me well. I find that I learn more by struggling through things versus being handed a playbook, and this time I was fully prepared to make this livelihood work!

BNI and PPA ended up being highly beneficial to me. I get sooooo nervous when I have to try to promote myself! I've met many amazing peers through these groups, and working with them has helped my nervousness immensely. I mean, I still get nervous... but it's better!

PPA is where I met other great photographers from the area, like Johnny Sundby, Russell Jensen and Ed Matuska. **(Read more about PPA and it's influence on me on page 192.)** Back when I'd been on a break from college, I'd visited Matuska's portrait studio and saw a plaque on the wall naming him a Master of Photography. I remember thinking, "Ooooh, that sounds cool, I wonder how you become a Master of Photography!" I didn't know Ed at the time so couldn't ask, but I finally found out the answer when I joined PPA – the master's degree and other achievements are earned through their national organization.

So I took on the PPA achievements with the same fervor I'd had on all of my photography adventures, and managed to surprise myself a few times over: I earned my Master of Photography and Photographic Craftsman honors after just three years of hard work, and I won the South Dakota PPA Photographer of the Year these last three years in a row, 2017-2019! Just at the start of 2020 I was giddy over winning my biggest honor to date, first place at PPA's Grand Imaging Awards, held that year in Nashville. My black and white composite image "Nothing Like Mom's Homemade Clam Chowder" **(see page 12)** took home first place in the landscape and nature category, chosen from thousands of images.

Being a self-employed photographer is not all sunshine and rainbows, of course. There's ups and downs, success and failure, much like all of life. I've found that I appreciate the struggles… they allow me to discover my own likes and style. I'm proud of what I've built, and what I get to share with the world.

DISCOVER WITH ME!
I love, love, love, LOVE what I do. I'm a travel-addicted photographer who gets high off the beauty of the world, and I hope to keep doing this photography thing for the rest of my life.

I truly hope you enjoy the photos and stories in this book. Thanks for going on this journey with me!

Portrait by Kevin Eilbeck

TIME TO *explore*

STORY TIME
I swear, it's all true! Crazy things tend to happen when you're chasing the light.

SOMETHING TO APPRECIATE

Morro Rock State Preserve | California, United States

EXPOSURE
Not Recorded (Hey, it was 1999!) | ISO 50

CAMERA GEAR
Nikon N90s | Black & White Ilford Pan F Plus Film

october 1999

I love my parents. They are amazing and so supportive of everything I do, and I wouldn't be where I'm at today without them.

But like many kids, I wasn't always appreciative of my parents. Especially when I was a teenager who'd just moved to big-time California from small-ish town South Dakota! This image comes from those days when I was all about getting into my cool new life pursuing an artsy career.

So when my parents came to visit during my freshman year in college, I wasn't too keen on the idea of playing tourist with them. I went, but with a bit of a crabby chip on my shoulder! I've thankfully left the attitude in the past, and I have this image as a reminder of how far I've come.

Back to the tour… our starting point was my college town of Santa Barbara, where Brooks Institute of Photography was located. We decided to head north up the coast on Highway 101 towards Hearst Castle, where my mom had called to get us tour reservations.

I do get to say I wasn't the only crabby one that day – my dad and I were both grumpy about going on a castle tour, even though, years later, we went and toured it without my mom! I'm guessing she's still not happy about that…

Anyway, the first town we stopped at was Morro Bay, where the stunning view of a gigantic rock sticking up like a sentinel out of the ocean caught our attention. It was a sight to see, especially on such a bright, sunny day!

We decided to stroll around the town and have lunch while we were there. We had just ordered our food when I turned to enjoy the view of Morro Rock. But I didn't get the view I expected!

In the middle of a bright, sunny day with a cloudless blue sky, a crazy fog was rolling in, only around the rock! My brain had to do a double take, and of course, I just had to capture this singular event. I looked at my parents, said "Sorry, I have to go do pictures!" and I ran outside.

The next thing I remember, my parents were outside, standing next to me with my lunch in a to-go box! How long had I been shooting?

Looking back I feel like a jerk for ditching my parents during lunch… but on the other hand, this is my passion and I've come to realize that when nature puts on a show, it's time for me to work.

Mom, Dad, I hope I've finally made up for my bratty years. Thank you for EVERYTHING you've done to help me follow my dreams!

B&W film strips, negative and reversed

Misty Mountain Fog Morro Rock, a volcanic plug, with a bank of eerie fog – Morro Bay, CA

October 1999

THE MOST WHAT THE F? STORY EVER

Bighorn Mountains | Wyoming, United States

EXPOSURE
Film speeds were 50 & 100... that's all I remember!

CAMERA GEAR
Nikon N90s | Velvia 50 & Kodak Supra 100 Film

august 2001

If there ever was a story that deserved to be in a book titled "What the F?" then this is it. This is one of those stories that was, until now, confidential to the two people involved. Even then, one small fact was kept secret from the other until only a few years ago… but I'm getting ahead of myself. Shall we start at the beginning? This is the story of how my friend Anna and I found ourselves being much more adventurous than we should have been!

During my medical break from college, I worked at Ritz Camera in the Rushmore Mall with my best friend Anna. We sold cameras and processed film. One day a college friend of Anna's brought in a roll of film that showed beautiful images of mountains after developing. I wanted to see those mountains! When the guy picked up his film we questioned him and found out he had just hiked Cloud Peak in the Bighorns, which is just a few hours west of the Black Hills in Wyoming.

The Bighorns were close enough for a weekend getaway, and that settled it! We decided a backpacking trip in the mountains was the perfect way to end my break and celebrate before I returned to school in September.

Had we ever been backpacking before? No. Had we ever hiked in the Bighorns before? Nope. Were we still going to go? You betcha!

I had some gear for camping and Anna's dad had a pack. That's a start! I mean, it's just hiking and camping, right? What could go wrong?

LOTS. Lots could go wrong. But again, I get ahead of myself… We did some research and acquired any missing gear, and we felt ready to face whatever the mountains could throw at us! Oh, the follies of youth...

The folly began with our parents trusting inexperienced 19-year-olds to go on this crazy adventure. Anna's mom had a bit less trust than mine and demanded that we carry a crap ton of water with us. (Even though I had just bought a $100 water purifier, but that didn't seem to matter…) We each carried at least a liter of water in our packs, plus cameras! We were only going to camp two nights, so for food we brought ramen, some bars, a few dehydrated food packs and Mentos (this is important later). We were set!

We even thought to bring a topography map with us, as we needed something to guide us on our hike. It is important to note that

▲ ▶ Infrared Slides
These are not Photoshopped – I didn't have Adobe back then, hadn't even gone digital yet!

See the end of the story for info on how infrared film works.

Alien Landscape The splendid beauty of Lost Twin Lakes, looking freaky via infrared film – Bighorn Mountains of Wyoming, USA   August 2001

NEITHER of us knew how to use it, or even had a compass … but hey, we had a map!

Another mishap came when we thought going out with friends the night before leaving was a GREAT idea, versus getting a good night's rest for the drive and hike the following day. What can I say - when you're that age you feel invincible, ready to take on the world.

So it was a bit tough getting going the next morning!

Thankfully the drive was uneventful - no speeding tickets this time like back on our High School graduation trip to Yellowstone, where just an hour in I was caught going a bit too fast and then ticketed by Wyoming Highway Patrol. I'm pretty sure that's why Anna said she would drive this time…

We managed to arrive at our trailhead at a decent time, still plenty of light. Doing good! We got all our gear loaded onto our backs… and from the looks on our faces we could tell each one of us was rethinking the choices we had made on what to carry! But not a peep was made: we were committed. Off to the trailhead!

As I remember it, I'd left the job of tracking trail numbers to Anna, so I trusted her to go the right way. Areas such as this usually have you fill out a card with the number of people in your party, length of stay and your destination and such, so they can make a plan if you don't return. As we were filling out our card to drop in the registration slot, an elderly volunteer ranger greeted us and asked where we were off to. We proudly proclaimed, "Lake Helen and Lake Mistymoon!" He was delighted and said, "Have a great time!" and then watched as we took a LEFT on the trails, and then went RIGHT down the next trail. You can guess where this story is heading, right?

The biggest blunder came when one trail was called something like trail 85 and the other was called trail 89… and we had picked the wrong one. In our defense, the numbers were newly carved in unstained and unpainted wood. Kinda hard to read! Plus, the RANGER should have said, "Hey girls, wrong trail!" but noooooo, he watched as we headed off 90 degrees in the WRONG direction.

◀ Color Slides ▼
Vivid blue hues pop in these slides from Lost Twin Lakes.

▲ Color Prints ▶
These are prints of Mirror Lake shot on my Nikon N90s...

Wow, I've come a long ways!

Now, as I said, we brought a map, but it was a topography map - a bit hard to read when one is not used to it, and REALLY hard to read when one does not realize they are on the WRONG TRAIL.

We had been hiking on fairly flat ground for 40-ish minutes when we came upon a waterfall. We took off our packs to enjoy the sight and rest because, you know, we had been hiking for… less than an hour. After a few snapshots we shouldered our packs and moseyed on. The trail followed the water's edge at first, but then about 30 minutes later the trail kept getting rougher… and less defined… and then it disappeared altogether! We finally concluded that yep, we had NOT been following the right trail. We had gotten ourselves lost.

We really did not feel like backtracking, so I pulled out the map and tried to find the waterfall we'd stopped at along the trail for Lake Helen. This was tough because, as you know, we were NOT on that trail. Anna was starting to panic, and I was desperately trying to find a solution, looking at the black and white lines and drawings denoting hills, meadows and water. Sooooo confusing!

After a while I proudly proclaimed that the trail was "This way!!!" I was basically pointing to the left up a hill. But if you can believe it, we actually made it back to the trail! I'm not sure how long it took… time slows down when you are lost and scared.

Once we found our feet back on the dirt path our spirits were lifted! Anna took extra comfort in how confident I looked: like I knew what I was doing, nothing to worry about here, la dee da! It was not until just a few years ago that I finally told Anna the TRUTH of how I "found" the trail.

You see, I had no idea where we were and was also panicked, but tried not to show it. I looked up to the sky and sent a plea into the world, asking for help… right when I had that thought, a bird landed in front of me and then took off to the left. I took THAT as a sign that "left and up the hill" was to be our heading, and by sheer dumb luck, it was!

Once we were back on the trail, we sat, allowing our nerves to calm. Then, miraculously, some people came down the trail and their son informed us we were almost there! Anna and I locked eyes, excited - we could not wait to set up camp! We threw our packs back on and headed off with our renewed spirits. As we crested the hill, we saw a lake situated among the trees. We thought it best to camp on the far side but were unsure if the trail followed the lake all the way around. We saw another couple headed our way and thought we'd ask them about it. I pulled out the map.

As they came closer we asked if this trail went to the other side of Lake Helen? The hikers looked very confused and said, "You mean… Mirror Lake."

I had a look of shock on my face, as did Anna. We gaped at each other and couldn't believe it… now we really had no idea where we were! I suspect we started grumbling at each other about what to do now, and the couple seemed concerned about whether they should leave us. Bucking up, we told them we would be fine. We quickly moved off the trail, looked closer at the map and discovered how things had gone horribly wrong from the beginning. We definitely weren't where we meant to be!

Well… this place was as good as any. We decided it was best if we just set up camp at Mirror Lake for the night.

Spirits were low but the beauty of Mirror Lake

▲
Color Negative Film Strips

Color negatives are ugly! It's amazing that reversing this nasty looking orange-y film produces normal color.

The orange strip is what color film looks like after it's developed, and the bottom strip is reversed to show the normal colors.

did wonders to boost our moods. We eventually laughed it off and were glad to at least know where we actually were. I would like to point out that at this point we were plenty exhausted… and had only hiked roughly 2.75 miles, a laughable feat. We were so unprepared for this trek! I repeat: I am not sure why our parents let us go! Perhaps they thought we would chicken out and get a hotel.

Now that our topographical map was a usable tool, we were able to see the trail we'd accidentally taken ended at Lost Twin Lakes. It looked pretty close, and we thought it would be perfect to hike without our packs in the morning. We could take just our camera bags to enjoy the day!

After a dinner of "styrofoam potatoes and dehydrated jerky that some people call beef stew" (how Anna described it in her journal later, ha!), we hit the hay. We opted for ramen instead of the dehydrated meals for breakfast, which tasted MUCH better and filled us up for the day's adventure.

Since we thought the lakes were close (curse you, topographical map) and we were, you know, ~invincible~, we didn't bring very much water or snacks. So once again we were not prepared for the day's venture… but thankfully the lakes at the end were sooooooo worth it.

▲ My 20-year-old boxes of infrared film

In fact, once we got our first view of the lakes, the beauty so elevated our mood we thought, "Why not hike around the lakes?" C'mon, that has to be a great idea!

In short, it was NOT. Our naive eyes could not properly understand the vast scale of the scene in front of us, and it turned out there wasn't even a trail. This lake was not more than a couple miles from our campsite, but this adventurous jaunt around the lakes had to have added two extra miles to our day. By the time we were almost back to the start of our little detour, we'd hiked more than the day before! We were hungry and thirsty. At this point I was dragging, just putting one foot in front of the other… and then I heard a voice behind me yell, "I am the greatest person in the world!" It was Anna of course, and she had discovered a pack of Mentos in her camera bag! Thankfully that dose of sugar gave us the boost we needed to get back on the actual trail and back to our tent.

All in all, this trip is the craziest and most stupid thing I have ever done, and I suspect Anna might say the same! Sooooo unprepared.

In our defense, we had no internet database like we have today for researching. No GPS on our phones. No articles with handy tips from those who had gone before us. Just our youthful spirit and a great deal of luck! I suspect now after reading this book our parents are going to have a bit to say… I hope they feel 19 years is enough time to protect one from being scolded! Statute of limitations? Sorry moms and dads.

I realize now I was so busy retelling this crazy story that I forgot to tell you about the crazy pink, blue and white picture that goes with it! **(See page 25.)** I had chosen to bring a roll of color infrared film with me on that trip - film that, even at that time, was difficult to come by. And difficult to shoot! So the fact I have images is extraordinary.

You see, this film is SO sensitive to light that it has to be removed from the film canister and loaded into the camera in COMPLETE darkness - and the same for getting the film out of the camera. I'm amazed I didn't get light leaks when I had to load the film with my hands and the camera simply shoved into a sleeping bag! Miraculous.

Infrared film is different because it reacts to light on the infrared spectrum, and the interpretive colors create surreal looking images. Nature is my favorite subject – the green color of plant life becomes a beautiful pink/red/magenta color, resulting from the density of chlorophyll in the subject. I thought with all the rocks in the Bighorns that the spruce trees would provide a stunning contrast, and I was not disappointed.

If you can believe it, I still have two rolls of infrared film in my fridge that have been with me since college. I had plans to shoot those last two rolls someday, but part of me just wants to hold on to them forever and imagine the possibilities. I try to finish all my "somedays" since, as anyone who knows me would have heard me say, "someday is code for never"… but just this once I might keep on dreaming.

The hiking misadventures of Erica & Anna!

"What can I say - when you're that age you feel invincible, ready to take on the world."

ROCKIN' the 90s grunge look

Soothing Santorini This blue domed church on the coast of Santorini caught my eye! – Greece

April 2006

THE TRIP THAT STARTED MY OBSESSION

Santorini, Greece

EXPOSURE
Shutter 1/100 sec. | Aperture f/5.6 | ISO 200

CAMERA GEAR
Nikon D2X | Nikkor 28-70 f/2.8 | Shot @ 42mm w/Crop Sensor

april 2006

I was fortunate to go on quite a few trips in my youth. I'd been to Disney World and Hawaii on family trips, and I'd even been to New Zealand on a high school foreign exchange trip, then to Costa Rica in college for a group documentary trip. But still, I didn't catch the travel bug until I took my first independent trip (apart from family or school) in 2006.

In 2005, one of my oldest childhood friends asked me to be the Maid of Honor at her wedding – and not just any wedding! The couple was eloping to Santorini, Greece. I instantly said YES! I had no idea how I was going to pay for it, I just knew I was going!

I came up with the idea to invite a couple of friends to travel with me and make the trip affordable for each of us. I'd go for the wedding, they'd go for a vacation! The plan was that we would head to Santorini a day early so I could enjoy some time with the wedding couple; then we'd head to Athens after the wedding for a grand tour that would take us through the Greek Isles, and back to Santorini again. It sounded perfect.

Mother Nature, it seemed, had other plans. A crazy late spring snowstorm shut down our little airport in Rapid City, and we were stuck! I was worried about getting a flight out in time, but we were thankfully able to catch one on the day of the ceremony. Whew!

It was still a close call though! I remember arriving in the evening and going straight from the airport to the hotel outside of town, then rushing to the room to get my dress on and hurrying to be in the wedding. There hadn't been time – or light! – to take in the sights, but the only view I needed that day was the beautiful scene of watching my friend marry her soul mate. I couldn't have been happier for them, and I was so glad to have made it in time.

The celebration after included more food than I've ever seen at any occasion! I swear we had about 36 different servings – it just kept coming! I eventually made my way back to the room, tired and STUFFED, only to find out... my friends, who didn't attend the wedding, hadn't eaten in over 24 hours.

We'd been rushing through airports all day with no time to eat and, much to my dismay, the wedding had shut down the hotel's restaurant for other guests! It was a small hotel and it was far enough on the outskirts that my friends hadn't been able to get back into town to eat after rushing me to the hotel. I felt terrible! But, unable to do anything, we gave in to exhaustion and slept.

The newlyweds took off on their honeymoon the next day, and we (after eating, of course) took off to Athens to begin the rest of our vacation! And THIS was why I'd brought my camera. The tour took us to so many beautiful sights, but I was surprised in the end that my favorite overall was our return trip to Santorini!

> "Travel... is like ... a first date."

When we'd first arrived, we really couldn't see the beauty of this island. My passion for photography was awakened by the beautiful white and blue architecture, contrasted by the moody sea in the background. All in all it was a wonderful trip, but this church in Santorini encompasses the best parts for me.

And just like that, my addiction to travelling had begun! Planning the trip myself - with photography in mind - sparked a desire to do it over and over again. Nothing brings me more joy than travelling and pursuing my passion... except maybe getting to share those experiences with loved ones.

Travel itself is like going on a first date: you don't know what to expect at first - you're not even sure you're going to like it! - but as you explore and discover more and more, you get to fall in love. Nothing reminds me of that joy like my photographs.

It has now been 14 years since this obsession began. I'm definitely an addict! Heck, I'm usually thinking of where I should go next before I even get home from the last trip! But hey, even though it's an expensive addiction, at least it's a healthy one, and I've made a happy career out of it.

BETTER THAN DREAMING IN BED

Devils Tower National Monument | Wyoming, United States

EXPOSURE
Shutter 1/80 sec. | Aperture f/16 | ISO 200

CAMERA GEAR
Nikon D2X | Nikkor 28-70 f/2.8 | Shot @ 57mm w/Crop Sensor

2007 *june*

Some may be surprised to learn that I'm not much of a morning person. This story is from early enough in my photography career that I had to work really, realllllly hard to get my butt out of bed. I especially struggle when it's my own cozy, comfy, wonderful bed at home!

Devils Tower National Monument is about a two-hour drive from my home in Rapid City, South Dakota. To make it out past the Wyoming border for a 5:30 sunrise at the monument in springtime, I'd need to be on the road by three-o-clock in the MORNING! Ugh…

So the alarm went off. I got up, used the restroom… and went back to bed. The drive sounded so awful (especially compared to my warm bed) and I just wasn't feeling it. I would only be disappointed with myself later… nobody else was expecting me to go capture sunrise in Wyoming. I could live with that.

Or so I thought. After laying there for 15 minutes and not being able to sleep, I had to give in to the nagging in my brain. Sleeping in wasn't worth the possibility of missing something epic at Devils Tower. So up I went! Grabbed my stuff, made sure my pup was fed (and gave her a jealous glare as she curled back up to sleep), and out the door I went.

It was completely dark for the drive up of course, and I couldn't even tell if the stars were showing. Was it cloudy? Wouldn't that just be my luck? But as I neared Sundance, the sky was getting light enough to see that it was clear. Not the best conditions for a sunrise photo – Give me big fluffy clouds! – but it was far better than being overcast.

So my hopes of epic-ness were low as I got closer to the monument. But what's this? As I rounded a hill the monument was still far away, but I was surprised to see that a huge layer of fog had settled at the base.

I was in for a treat!

The experience shooting that morning was wonderfully unexpected, and I got images I hadn't even thought to dream of. The distinctive volcano core started as a silhouette peeking through the mist, and as the sun rose the crags became defined and I captured this image. Soon after that the fog burned off, disappearing as if it hadn't been there at all.

This is one of my favorite images of Devils Tower to this day. Every time I head up to shoot sunrise at the monument, I hope that I'll get the fog bank again. The D2X camera was only 12MP, so I'm hoping to get lucky one day and do it justice with a camera that will let me print it BIG!

◀ Magical fog at Devils Tower ▼

The Devils Misty Shroud The distinct rock formation rising out of a mysterious cloud bank – Devils Tower National Monument, USA

June 2007

Waking Up the Sky Nearly missed sunrise light at Swift Current Lake – Glacier National Park, USA

July 2007

WHEN IN DOUBT, GET UP AND GO

Glacier National Park | Montana, United States

EXPOSURE
Shutter 1.3 sec. | Aperture f/16 | ISO 160

CAMERA GEAR
Nikon D2X | Nikkor 17-35 f/2.8 | Shot @ 28.5mm w/Crop Sensor

2007 july

As you just learned in the last story, I'm not really a morning person. I would much rather sleep in, burrowed in the comfy-ness of my warm bed, than drag myself out into the chilly morning air. But as any good photographer knows, some of the best light happens at sunrise. That means EARLY, while everyone else is still cuddled in bed. Sigh…

This image was taken early on in my professional photography career while I was on a trip with my mom. I almost didn't get it because – yep, you guessed it – this light happened early in the morning.

Even though I hadn't yet discovered my passion for epic sunrises at that age, I was still aware of the importance of capturing the best light. So I diligently set my alarm in the hotel the night before. Best intentions, right? And when it went off in the morning, I DID get up! I didn't need to set the alarm for too terribly early because our hotel was literally right by this lake, and my window even looked right out at this view. I could easily check the conditions for photography.

And the conditions were… overcast. Bleh. Oh well, back to the warm, cozy bed!!!

> "What if you miss something AMAZING?"

Next thing I know as I'm nestled in fluffy blankets and pillows, I hear a bunch of voices outside. "What the heck is going on?" I thought. Curious, I dragged myself back out of bed. Lo and behold, there's a bunch of photographers setting up to shoot! I thought to myself, "What are they thinking? Nothing's going to happen. What a waste of time." Aaaaaaand I happily crawled back in to bed.

But then my brain wouldn't shut up. There was this little voice in my head nagging me with "What-ifs?" and "How stupid will you feel if you're wrong?" Then, "What if you miss something AMAZING?!?!"

So I got up for the third time, finally got dressed, and headed out the door. I cruised right by the group to find my own unique spot of course. I had just barely set up when the sun peaked through and created this wonderful moment. This light lasted about one minute, and it was done. I was in awe.

I learned a valuable lesson that morning: when in doubt, always get out of bed. And this lesson applies to life in general! If you're doubting something, it's probably worth at least trying. Listen to that little voice in your head, and perhaps you'll be rewarded with something amazing.

THE SADNESS BEHIND THE BEAUTY

Mosi-oa-Tunya National Park | Zambia, Africa

EXPOSURE
Shutter 1/640 sec. | Aperture f/5.6 | ISO 400

CAMERA GEAR
Nikon D2X | Nikkor 28-70 f/2.8 | Shot @ 105mm w/Crop Sensor

march 2008

Back in 2008 when I went to Africa with my sister, I was only an amateur photographer. I was still learning my style and discovering who I was as an artist. I wish I could go back with my new gear and knowledge, but for where I was at the time, I feel I got some pretty good images.

This rhinoceros image in particular did not resonate with me originally because it wasn't what I envisioned at the time; however, I've grown to appreciate the experience that came with it, and what it now means to me.

I had paid for a tour called a "Rhino Walk," and the photo I envisioned was of a rhinoceros in the grass with a beautiful Africa vista in the background. Well, it turned out the "vista" part was going to be impossible in our area. We happened to be so near Victoria Falls that all the extra moisture meant there was a LOT of heavy vegetation. So instead of African plains in the background, we got shrubs. Yaaayyyy...

The vegetation was so dense that it was actually hard to even see the rhino at first. But the tour guide apparently spotted him and dropped us off on the road "near" the rhino, then parked the truck a little ways off. We wandered in the direction they indicated, still not seeing the rhino.

I mean, how can you not see a RHINO?

The behemoth eventually emerged from the grass, and for a second we were excited to see him better... but then I suddenly realized I was almost close enough to TOUCH this massive creature! I was too close to even take a full picture (see the picture below). I was cringing in my head because I like to try and respect an animal's boundaries. We were definitely invading his space!!!

I was utterly surprised the guides would get us this close to a wild animal, but it turned out they had good reason not to worry. This particular rhino was completely used to people and, as a result of tourism, didn't seem to mind strangers being so close.

My sister & I with nervous smiles, uncomfortably close to a RHINO!

Is it just me, or are we WAY too close?!?

The Lonely White Rhino A lonely white rhino, after losing his friend to poaching – Mosi-oa-Tunya National Park, Africa

March 2008

He happened to be the last of his kind in the park, a rare white rhino, so he was protected by guards 24/7. Since the park needed funds for such an enterprise, they allowed frequent trips of tourists to visit and check him out. All of this made the rhino uncommonly comfortable with people.

Sadly, there's only so much that can be done to protect the rare and unique animals of the world. Not long before we arrived, the only other rhino like this guy in the park had been killed for his horn.

Poaching is a major problem in Africa, particularly for the tusks of elephants and rhino's horns. It saddened me to see this majestic creature left alone in the world, just because someone wanted to sell his parts for profit on the black market.

> "We should never stop fighting to change the world."

Even though I didn't get to photograph my epic African landscape, I still did my best to photograph the rhino. This was the image I processed, but I was pretty "meh" about it and didn't finish it at the time.

Something must have nagged me about the image though, because I revisited it and processed it in black and white. It made all the difference, and the image struck a chord with me. I feel the black and white treatment lends itself to the sad story behind this animal's life, giving it more meaning and interest. It represents the reason we should never stop fighting to change the world.

I also learned that time can completely change how we feel about a piece of art. It never hurts to take another look!

Eye Zeeee You The zebra I annoyed... sorry dude! – Mosi-oa-Tunya National Park, Africa

March 2008

PUSHING BOUNDARIES

Mosi-oa-Tunya National Park | Zambia, Africa

EXPOSURE		CAMERA GEAR
Shutter 1/100 sec.	Aperture f/5.6	ISO 400		Nikon D2X	Nikkor 70-300 f/4.5-5.6	450mm w/Crop Sensor

march 2008

This image was taken early on in my career as I was working on building my portfolio. I was excited for my sister's and my trip to Africa, and ecstatic at the idea of photographing the unusual (to me) landscapes and exotic animals!

I had all sorts of glorious visions in my head of the images I wanted to capture, such as extreme close-ups of wild animals. My Nikon D2X camera had 1.5 magnification that gave me a 450mm range, but it still got me nowhere near as close as I wanted to be to the animals out in the field.

I still did my best and got some amazing shots on the camera, but as the end of the trip neared I just didn't have the close-up feel that I wanted. Then on our last full day in Africa, I happened to look out our patio door to see a small group of zebras munching on the hotel ground's fresh cut grass! It turns out that Mosi-oa-Tunya Park has no predators, so the animals were not shy around people and often wandered onto the grounds.

I knew this was my chance! I headed out with my camera and slowly approached the herd. I would snap a couple shots, then move a little closer. When I moved in and snapped this shot, the zebra kind of huffed at me. I was like, "OK, I found the edge of your bubble, I'll stop. Please, just don't charge at me…"

It was a stupid move because even though grazing animals like zebra seem docile, they are still wild and can charge you in a split second. And rightfully so. It's happened back home with the bison in our state park (thankfully not too often), and it's always because a tourist overstepped their bounds. And here I was, a tourist in Africa, overstepping my bounds. If you're close enough to change the animal's behavior, such as making them eye you or huff or snort, then you're too close.

And the worst part is that when someone gets injured by an animal charge, the animal might be the one who pays. We've all heard stories in the news where an innocent animal was euthanized for it's natural behavior.

As a nature photographer, conservation is my first concern, and the animals should always come first. I keep this in mind on all of my shoots and do my best to respect the animals' space. Of course, better gear helps!

The many adventures of the Johnson sisters in Africa! ▶

A BIG SURPRISE

Yellowstone National Park | Wyoming, United States

EXPOSURE
Shutter 1/320 sec. | Aperture f/11 | ISO 100

CAMERA GEAR
Nikon D610 | Nikkor 28-70 f/2.8 | Shot @ 42mm

2014 may

It was a beautiful day in Yellowstone National Park. The sky was blue, the clouds were wispy… and the crazy people were out. Woo hoo!

I was exploring the boardwalks around Old Faithful Geyser that afternoon, and as I walked the upper loop I came upon a large bison with his rump pressed right up against the boardwalk. I knew better and wasn't going to risk getting gored by passing the behemoth and possibly upsetting him, so I walked the upper boardwalk instead.

But I also know how tourists act around the buffalo back home in the Black Hills of South Dakota… and I thought to myself, "Well, this might get interesting."

The journalist in me decided to hunker down with my camera in the hopes of catching a tourist getting gored. I know, sounds morbid, but seriously… I've seen people repeatedly get too close to the "big fluffy cows" back home, even after repeated warnings from the rangers, so I wasn't going to waste my time trying to warn off every Tom, Dick and Harry. Might as well see what happens and take advantage of the situation. I mean, don't all photographers want their picture on the front page?

It didn't take long for the crazy parade to start. Instead of turning around and going back the long way to avoid the big bison, people just strolled right past him. Seeing the buffalo seemingly "not react," people just kept on coming. I shook my head. I'm scared of any big grazing animals - they're unpredictable! One minute they're calm, and then all of a sudden you could have a horn stuck in your side.

Parents were even going back for pictures with their KIDS, placing children on the edge of the boardwalk, just feet away from the bison's massive head!

Eventually he'd had enough and hopped up onto the boardwalk – that made a few people jump – and he moseyed away. Darn, no Pullitzer Prize for me today.

As I got up though, there was a roar behind me…

I turned and discovered a geyser was about to erupt! (You were thinking someone was finally going to get gored, weren't you?)

It turned out I was meant to get stuck on the boardwalk that day. I was about to see Lion Geyser go off in all its glory, and it was one of the few geysers I'd never seen erupt before! The sun was right in my eyes, but it ended up beautifully backlighting the steam and water from the eruption, and I captured this dynamic image. I had no idea how long the gush would last and I probably could have zoomed out to get the whole eruption in frame, but no matter. This image and that day will always stand out in my mind, even if I didn't make the front page news.

Not afraid of the big fluffy boulder ▼

Lion's Misty Mane Lion Geyser puts on its first show for me – Yellowstone National Park, USA

May 2014

A GLOOMY AND GRIZZLY EXPERIENCE

Grand Teton National Park | Wyoming, United States

EXPOSURE
Shutter 1/500 sec. | Aperture f/5.6 | ISO 500

CAMERA GEAR
Nikon D610 | Nikkor 200-400 f/4.0 | 560mm w/ TC-14E II

2014 may

It sometimes turns out that when I'm the most disappointed in the weather, I end up with the best shots.

I arrived at Colter Bay in the Tetons around 11:30 pm with a 5:30 am sunrise ahead of me. As soon as I got the essentials out of my vehicle I tried to get some rest, but of course was too amped up from shooting earlier. Needless to say, it didn't feel like I'd been sleeping long when the alarm was telling me it was time to get up. It was 4:45 am. I'll be honest… I wanted to stay in bed. I was quite tired from the previous day and when I looked out the window, I couldn't see any sign of the sky – just dull, boring grey clouds.

So I laid there, 99% sure I was going to say "Screw it!" and get more sleep… but then a little voice said, "If you don't get up, you're going to miss it!" Miss what I did not know, but as always the competitive side of me couldn't let other photographers grab the shot while I was wasting my morning in bed. So I got up, grabbed my clothes, pulled on a hat and out the door I went.

As I pulled out of Colter Bay, I looked to the sky and realized that what I thought were clouds was actually fog… and heavy fog, at that. Which meant: NO mountains, NO trees, NO blue sky, NO white puffy clouds, NO sunrise shot. I contemplated my next step… then I noticed what looked to be a mountains peeking out at the southern end of the park. Could I get there in time? Where would I shoot? So many choices, and the decision had to be made in seconds. I took a gamble and raced off to hopefully find a spot and catch whatever Mother Nature provided for sunrise.

Now, understand… I had not been to the park since 2004 (except for a quick drive through in 2011), and since it was 2014 I was unfamiliar with the roads and had no idea where I was going to end up. The good news was my gamble paid off and the mountains were visible! But the sun was rising fast. I quickly pulled into the first turnout I could find. It would not have been my first choice but I made do and created a panoramic. It wasn't the image I had set out to create, but it was still a beautiful moment.

Aaaaaaaaaaand here comes the What the f? part.

During the course of shooting the pano, the unthinkable happened. My camera started flashing "Card Error!" No! I had never had this happen before and started to panic. Thankfully I was able to keep myself together and calmly took the card out, sticking in a new one to finish up my shot.

This is one of those moments where I wished I'd used a backup card, but I just never got in the habit. I guess I like living on the dangerous side, ha! I normally would have kept on heading down the road, but all I could think about was my card. Did my card just crash? Had all previous 1,000 images been erased?

Panic began to set in, so I got in my car and raced back to the hotel. With luck, I could at least transfer the files and have peace of mind that I had copies. I was just five minutes away from my cabin when I started to cross the Jackson Lake Dam and I saw a few cars pulled over. Being the good tourist/

Panoramic of Tetons scenery ▼

Hey Boo Boo Momma bear, a.k.a. Grizzly Bear #399 (some creative naming, right there), and her cub – Grand Teton National Park, USA   MAY 2014

photographer that I am and knowing that stopping for a few minutes wouldn't impact the possibly errored-out card, I pulled over to see what was going on.

At first I could not see what all the fuss was about… but then, there it was, a grizzly bear! In fact, it was the first bear I had ever seen in the Tetons.

I was beyond excited, and then became even more excited when I found out she was a mom and had what looked to be two little cubs along! Baby bears!!! I soon forgot all about my card problems and grabbed the BIG lens. This sucker is so big that without a tripod, I had to prop the lens on my car door and try not to breathe to avoid camera shake.

I didn't expect to get the best shots since the sage grass they were situated in was very tall, and the bears were very interested in eating the short green grass underneath. So their heads were down. A lot. I took a few shots but wanted to get away from the crowd, so I took a chance and moved my car to a different spot. It seemed she was going to head my direction! I got excited as I saw mom and cubs head straight for my car!

But… sadly the new location was not working. All three of the bears were now perfectly hidden in the sage. Ugh.

Then all of a sudden, mama bear popped up! I thought, "This is it, the money shot!" When she stood fully, I realized her BACK was turned to me. My heart sank instantly. Really? Why me? My first grizzly and this happens…. wait a minute, what's that moving next to her…

Next thing I knew a cub popped up right next to mom!!! I was able to get ONE frame with them standing with their backs perfectly facing me (gotta love those fuzzy ears). Then just like that they moved and the moment was over; the grizzlies headed away and the ranger showed up to get all us curious humans to move along.

But that's OK. I got my shot.

What happened to the card that led to this adventure, you ask? It was fine and I luckily retrieved the images, but the mama and baby bear photo that I titled "Hey Boo Boo" is the winning photo of the trip. Yay!

YEAH, SURE, COWS...

Grand Teton National Park | Wyoming, United States

EXPOSURE
Shutter 1/320 sec. | Aperture f/8 | ISO 500

CAMERA GEAR
Nikon D610 | Nikkor 70-200 f/4.0 | Shot @ 200mm

May 2014

It seemed I was blessed with wildlife photo opps on my 2014 trip exploring the Grand Tetons. This story took place on the same day that I captured my "Hey Boo Boo" image **(see the Gloomy and Grizzly story, previous page)**. I feel very lucky at what I captured that day.

▲ Cunningham Cabin panoramic with a Tetons backdrop

I was packed up and ready to head to my next location, Dinosaur National Monument. I left myself some time to explore on the way down, hoping to check out some places I'd never seen before. One area I particularly wanted to visit was Mormon Row – remnants of historic farms and homesteads built in the Tetons by a group of Mormons in the 1890s. I'm not a fan of man-made structures, but I make an exception for old barns. They're just so rustic and neat! Old barns and bridges are pretty much the only architecture I love to shoot artistically.

I first stopped at another historic building on the way down, Cunningham Cabin. I was working the scene and another photographer happened to join me. We exchanged pleasantries and went about our business. As I left, however, the gentleman yelled something to me. I thought it was something about a… cow? I asked again and it sounded like the same thing, something about a cow.

I wasn't sure why he thought he needed to tell me about cows; I live by plenty of cows and don't care to shoot cows in the Tetons! So as not to seem rude (and so I wouldn't look like an idiot), I decided to let him think I knew what he was saying. I was heading the direction he indicated anyway, so I was sure I could figure out if there was something interesting going on with cows! I waved thanks and headed out to Mormon Row (and possibly some cows).

When I finally turned down the correct road and approached the famous barns, I was excited to say the least. I'd missed seeing Mormon Row on my first trip to the Tetons and was looking forward to exploring the buildings and finding my shot.

◀◀ Aw! Sleepy pups at Mormon Row

Pile of Puppies A fuzzy ball of coyote pups snoozing by an old barn, soaking up the sun – Grand Teton National Park, USA

May 2014

I parked and found the place fairly quiet except for one tour van, and they were packing up to leave. I loaded up my gear when one of the ladies on the tour saw my camera and approached me. "I see you have a nice camera," she said. "I just have to tell you about a great photo opportunity over there!" She pointed to one of the smaller buildings.

Her explanation made my jaw drop. Apparently there was a group of coyote pups out sunning at the base of the building! Then it clicked – THAT'S what the photographer at Cunningham Cabin was trying to tell me! Not about cows, but coyotes!

I thanked the lady and hurried over. I was so glad she told me about them, or I could have completely missed them! It was cuteness overload, though a bit challenging to shoot when they're all piled up together. I love trying to count the pups in this shot. How many do you see?

FRIENDS KEEP US MOTIVATED

Banff National Park | Alberta, Canada

EXPOSURE
Shutter 27 sec. | Aperture f/13 | ISO 100

CAMERA GEAR
Nikon D610 | Nikkor 17-35 f/2.8 | Shot @ 26mm

2014 July

If ever there was a location that stole my heart, it would be the Canadian Rockies.

I'd seen pictures of the far-north Rocky Mountains a long time ago, but my best friend Toni had never heard of Banff National Park until she went to a film festival in Rapid City. She called me soon after and enthusiastically told me, "We have to go!" I said, "I know."

She didn't know how serious I was! I started planning us a 12-day trek through the Canadian Rockies, from Banff all the way to Jasper. Any time I head to a new location for photography, I try to find tips from local photographers on where to shoot and when the best light hits that location. I had every day planned out, and my bestie was more than happy to tag along.

We flew into Calgary and rented a car for the duration of our trip. As we made our way out of the city and headed into the mountains, my heart dropped. Smoke! I'd heard about a fire breaking out in the Banff area, but I was hoping they would get it put out quickly and that the smoke would dissipate. Not the case. Our first day in the town of Banff, you couldn't see the mountains. At all.

I tend to get depressed when I plan a photo trip and arrive to see that all my plans may go to waste. I especially get upset at something as destructive as a fire that's possibly caused by someone tossing a cigarette out the window, or something just as careless. I was ready to hunker down in the hotel room and just be sad.

But Toni was having none of it! She dragged my butt out the door and we explored the town. A soft rain moved in and slowly, the smoke began to dissipate! We even hiked the local hill on the edge of town. (Though compared to what we're used to, it felt like a mountain!) At the top we were able to see a view of the town and faint outlines of mountains bigger than we could have imagined.

Despite a successful few days of photography after that, I still had a hard time getting fully motivated on our trip. The next stop was the iconic Lake Louise area, and we arrived late in the afternoon. We couldn't wait to see the pretty lake, so before even checking

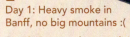

▲
Day 1: Heavy smoke in Banff, no big mountains :(

Day 2: Better, plus a smile!!! ▶

Day 3: Gondola on Sulfer Mtn. above Banff, a view clear of smoke! :) ▶▶

Morning's Blaze A few minutes of fiery morning light (NOT an actual fire) at Lake Louise – Banff National Park, Canada July 2014

out our accommodations, we ventured up the road to take in the scene and get an idea of where I could shoot from.

I'd tried to avoid seeing pictures of Lake Louise ahead of time, but it's so popular that it had popped up several times while I planned the trip. Now, seeing it in person? Whole different experience.

We'd lucked out and got a good parking spot, as most people were starting to head out for the day. You can't see the lake as you walk up from the lot – the trees block the view. I was stunned when we finally got a clear view of this expanse of teal-green glacial water nestled between tall glacially carved peaks… it was huge! Truly, pictures cannot do this gem of nature justice.

Could one ask for a more picturesque scene?

Well, yes… for photography, anyway! I'd planned four nights in the area to give myself ample opportunity to try and capture amazing sunrise and sunset light at both Lake Louise and nearby Moraine Lake. We ended up staying at the most adorable location, just minutes from either lake, so it would be super easy to get up for the early sunrise. It was summer, so that meant getting up by 4 am when you're that far north.

EXPOSURE Shutter 4 sec. | Aperture f/22 | ISO 100 **CAMERA GEAR** Nikon D610 | Nikkor 17-35 f/2.8 | Shot @ 24mm

Glacial Reflections A different sunrise at Lake Louise's neighbor, the stunning Moraine Lake – Banff National Park, Canada

On our last morning in the area we woke up and it was heavily overcast. I just wanted to crawl back into bed – hey, I'd already caught the last three sunrises! My lack of motivation was kicking in at the sight of a gloomy sky. Luckily Toni somehow had motivation - she's not normally a morning person but put her in Banff and she's rarin' to go! She tempted me out of bed with the promise that she'd somehow find me a latte.

I dragged myself out of bed and we took off for Lake Louise. Once there I set up, but I wasn't expecting much. Toni wandered off in search of coffee, and she thankfully didn't have to go far. You wouldn't know it from any of the pictures, but right behind the main vantage point there's a HUGE hotel. (It's really expensive to stay there, I checked.) It was chilly so I perked up once I had a steamy, caffeinated beverage in my system.

And good thing too! As we were enjoying our coffees, we were shocked to see a bright strip of light break through the clouds and light up the peaks! I put down my latte (don't worry, it was mostly gone) and started shooting as the fiery strip of light moved along the mountain. My favorite shot of that sunrise is "Morning's Blaze" on the previous page.

It lasted just a matter of minutes, and then it was raining cats and dogs! We packed up and raced back to our car, and back to our warm cozy beds.

The moral of the story? Get up and get moving, even if everything has you down. For you see, epic doesn't just happen on sunny days.

> "Epic doesn't just happen on sunny days."

Coffee helps! ▲

◄ After sunrise, after the rain... we went hiking for 9.5 hours!!!

HOW TO PISS OFF TOURISTS

Banff National Park | Alberta, Canada

EXPOSURE
Shutter 2.0 sec. | Aperture f/22 | ISO 125

CAMERA GEAR
Nikon D610 | Nikkor 17-35 f/2.8 | Shot @ 30mm

2014 july

As I mentioned in the last story, any time I travel to a new area, I do my research! I try to find out what I can about the best spots for a great experience and amazing photo opps. But research can't prepare you for everything.

Johnston Canyon is a popular spot in Banff National Park. It's not far off the highway with a nice parking area and general store, and you can choose from a shorter hike to the Lower Falls, a longer hike to Upper Falls, and a day hike even further to a valley with sulfurous pools (not worth the distance, IMO). For my first time on the hike my goal was to shoot a waterfall, so I loaded up the tripod and my friend Toni and I headed out late in the morning.

We soon discovered that the unique traverse up the canyon is what makes this hike a number one destination for tourists. You see, while much of the hike is above the ravine that the powerful stream has cut and carved through the mountain, a good portion of the trail actually descends INTO the canyon! The winding trail is a narrow, constructed walkway that is attached (securely, though it doesn't always look it...) to the side of the ravine.

It's a joyful trek, even more so when you have the trail to yourself. But this is a tourist hot spot, and as the day goes on, more and more people pile on to the trail, often resulting in single file lines of people marching along the long stretches of walkway.

In fact, most of the spots where you'd want to stop and take a photo are at narrow spots or on the walkways. This makes it a bit difficult to maneuver with a big camera bag,

▲ A Johnston Canyon walkway

much less set up a tripod! But a tripod is a MUST for a gorgeous, long-exposure waterfall image with beautifully blurred water.

A big photo tip for this area is to arrive as early as the light allows and try to beat the crowd! Of course, since this was our first time in the area... we didn't do that.

As soon as we reached Upper Falls, I knew this was where I wanted to shoot. Since the ravine is narrow, park designers were kind enough to create a stairway that descends almost all the way to the bottom of the canyon. They also built a metal walkway that takes you out over the water. At the end of the platform, you finally get a stunning view of the waterfall around a cliff that otherwise blocks the view.

The metal walkway is a bit narrow, of course, so hikers were kindly taking turns viewing the waterfall from the end of the platform. Luckily foot traffic that day wasn't too bad, so I patiently waited for the prime spot at the end of the walkway to free up, then promptly sent Toni to hold the spot!

As I unloaded my gear and got the tripod ready, I already knew I was in trouble. More and more people were coming down the stairs to get a look at the waterfall. I quickly took my friend's spot and got fully set up. After a few shots I had my two second exposure down and was ready to attach the graduated filter and start shooting! Yes!

But wait... what is that I feel? Oh crap! This platform is moving with every step and twitch a person makes, and it keeps shaking as they walk off the metal grate... there's so many people I can't even get two seconds of stillness!

I valiantly tried to get a good shot between tourists popping down for the prime waterfall view, but after 10 minutes I

Hang on Tight Johnston Canyon, Upper Falls: a glacial waterfall and some brave, brave trees! – Banff National Park, Canada   July 2014

still didn't have a sharp image and a line of people were forming, waiting for me to move.

All right, time to buck up! I charmingly (I think) explained to people that I needed just a few seconds with nobody on the platform to get my shot, so please, please, please wait! But as soon as I would get a group of people on board to wait, someone else would come along and push past onto the walkway, messing up the shot.

Then more people would squeeze in to look. And by this time the spray from the waterfall had splattered my filter. (Note to self: do a better job of blocking the water!) But I kept shooting. And shooting. And shooting.

I definitely succeeded in pissing off the tourists! Eventually my persistence paid off and I was able to get the above shot. This was an instance where, out of many, many shots, I had only ONE good frame that finally nailed it!

So the moral of this story is to always get to your location as early as possible to avoid crowds of angry tourists! And learn how to nicely stand your ground against whatever the situation might throw at you.

One last thing I would like to point out about my image "Hang on Tight" – you likely noticed the title of the image has nothing to do with the waterfall or water at all! When I took this photo, my focus was on those amazing little trees clinging to that cliff for dear life, and still managing to grow.

I thought these trees showed a great lesson: no matter what you are given in life, as long as you do NOT give up you CAN succeed. So in short, I stuck to my guns and took this image to showcase those wonderful trees. The lovely blurred waterfall was just an extra element that made this photograph more interesting.

NO TIME FOR INSURANCE

Jasper National Park | Alberta, Canada

EXPOSURE
Shutter 1/250 sec. | Aperture f/6.3 | ISO 500

CAMERA GEAR
Nikon D610 | Nikkor 70-200 f/4 | Shot @ 75mm

2014 july

This image really has nothing to do with the main part of this story, but it's all I've got to represent what happened.

This was my first trip to the Canadian Rockies. The final leg of the journey would take my friend Toni and me up north to the town of Jasper, and there were several locations in the area that I wanted to shoot. I was most excited about Angel Glacier near Mount Edith Cavell; I'd seen awesome pictures of this little glacial lake with icebergs and a distinct sprawling glacier above, shaped like an angel with wings.

I wanted to capture sunrise, so my travel buddy Toni and I set our alarms to get up crazy early on the second-to-last day of our trip (the sun was up well before 5 am). At first it seemed our day was going to be a bust – it was foggy outside and we'd slept through our alarms, and we wouldn't make it to the glacier in time for a sunrise photo. I thought it would still be fun to go check it out and find a shoot spot for the next morning, so we headed out into the gloomy fog.

The road to Mt. Edith Cavell ascends on its way out of town, and we were treated to the most amazing view. We were above the fog and the valley to the right had thousands of trees poking through, and the morning light just made the scene magical! I found a spot to pull off by the guard rail and shot as quickly as I could. (Thankfully it was early enough that there was only one other car on the road.) I shot to my heart's content, and then it was onward to Angel Glacier. This day way looking up!

Near the trail the road had a section of new concrete, and the parking lot was a mix of dirt and some rubble – it looked like there must have been a landslide at some point. I wondered if that happened a lot in this area and hoped the road was OK. There was nobody around, which is great, but we also had no cell reception if something happened. Made me think of how there's also a lot of bears in that area… but we weren't so far out of town that we were taking any great risks. So we parked, grabbed our gear, and headed up the trail!

▲ **Looks sturdy...**

▲ What a lovely picture of me on such a doomed day!

It was beautiful of course, even though we'd missed sunrise. The morning was so calm and quiet that the pool reflected the glacier crisp and clear. We made our way down to the edge of the lake, careful not to disturb our surroundings. I looked around and saw more signs of rock falls and landslides. What a neat area, I thought… and silently hoped that no rocks would fall on us or bears would sneak up on us. Don't worry! We were safe and had our bear spray, but that doesn't mean I want to use it!

I grabbed some test shots and found my spot, then unloaded my gear. I got my tripod set up, keeping the legs short to go for an extreme angle of the glacier, then attached my camera. As I turned to get my filters out of my camera bag, I heard a noise behind me! I quickly looked around, my heart skipping a beat as my helpful brain told me a bear must have shifted some ground while trying to sneak up on us…

It seemed like it happened in slow motion. As I finished turning, I watched, helpless, as my professional camera seemed to slowly and gracefully dive lens-first into a rock and disappear

Shrouded In Silence Foggy trees outside the town of Jasper... a gloomy portent of things to come? – Jasper National Park, Canada   July 2014

into the water. Thousands of dollars' worth of equipment was quickly and entirely submerged.

I swear my heart completely stopped for a second.

Not gonna lie, I full-on panicked. I had NEVER had this happen. I leaped to the water's edge and quickly yanked out my camera. I think I must have yelled for Toni because she stared at me, astonished, as I stripped off my outer layers, down to a tank top (it was pretty chilly out), so I could use my shirts to wipe up as much water as possible. How had this happened? I ALWAYS keep one hand on the tripod! My hands were shaking, and Toni gave me a worried glance. She'd never seen me so panicked. I glanced to the cursed spot by the water and noticed that while I'd set my tripod legs all on solid rocks, the ground under one of the rocks had given way. Ugh.

I packed up my camera bag faster than I ever have in my life and ran for my car, Toni scrambling after me. Thankfully I'd seen videos online full of hacks for what to do with electronics that get wet. We raced to the local grocery store to buy rice. Back at our room, I shoved the camera and lens into a sock and stuck it in a big bowl of the rice. I was still shaking, and I remembered something ironic – my mom had suggested I buy insurance just before the trip, but I'd been short on time and hadn't gotten around to it. Double ugh.

This also meant the photography part of my trip was over. To get my mind off things we explored Maligne Canyon that day. I tried some shots with Toni's hobbyist D7000 Nikon, but it just wasn't the same.

Things thankfully ended up OK. We spent our last day driving the Icefields Parkway, getting in an epic hike at Parker's Ridge and canoeing at Moraine Lake, which was a pretty great end to our adventure. My lens surprisingly survived with no technical issues, just a dinged edge for a battle scar. And my camera was able to get fixed for just $325, which is pretty awesome considering it's worth.

You would think I'd learned my lesson from this wonderful experience, but it still took yet another incidence of breaking my camera before I finally stopped procrastinating and bought insurance. Trust me, professional gear is worth protecting!

Now? I never leave home without insurance!

SUNRISE WITH PRESIDENTS AND STRANGERS

Mount Rushmore National Memorial | The Black Hills, South Dakota

EXPOSURE
Shutter 0.4 sec. | Aperture f/25 | ISO 400

CAMERA GEAR
Nikon D610 | Nikkor 70-200 f/4.0 | Shot @ 85mm

august 2014

As pictures of Mount Rushmore go, it can be difficult to create something unique and different. The lovely pink sunrise and sunset light known as alpenglow is one of my absolute favorite displays of nature's beauty, so to make this monumental picture my own I decided to shoot early in the morning and try to capture the faces bathed in this soft rosy light.

I had never been to Mount Rushmore at such an early hour, and I assumed I would be the only one there. I mean, what tourist would get up to go to Mount Rushmore in the dark?

As I left the parking lot and headed up towards the Avenue of Flags, I heard footsteps behind me. I glanced quickly around and saw a shadowy figure, which I decided could only be a night ranger. I mean… I assumed "night rangers" were a thing. Why not? So I kept on going and reached the edge of the amphitheater, the best viewpoint to see all of Mount Rushmore. This was where I would get my shot!

Next thing I knew… someone was standing next to me. And nope, not a ranger!

I instantly got nervous – I was a petite woman alone in a dark, secluded area, AND I was carrying valuable gear. It's sad, but even in a relatively safe area like the Black Hills, a person all alone can still have reason to worry. You just don't know that person and their intentions.

He of course chatted with me and seemed nice enough… he said he was from Hot Springs and had never been to Mount Rushmore, and had decided sunrise would be the

Tough Enough to Wear Pink Early morning with the presidents (multi-image panoramic) - Mount Rushmore National Memorial, USA   August 2014

EXPOSURE Shutter 1/13 sec. | Aperture f/22 | ISO 400   **CAMERA GEAR** Nikon D610 | Nikkor 28-70 f/2.8 | Shot @ 28mm

Road of Possibilities From sunshine to fog: a tree off a country road, shortly after the Rushmore sunrise - Black Hills of South Dakota, USA   August 2014

best for his first experience. Innocent as that sounded, I still had alarms going off in my head. I'd lived in a big coastal city, and I wasn't under the illusion that being in "small town middle-America" made me safe from predators.

While keeping up the chit chat, I texted a friend who I knew would be up early getting ready for work and asked if I could call them. While nervously waiting for a response, I mentioned to the stranger that the trail off to the left had some amazing views of the presidents, nice and close, and that he should be sure to go and explore the walkway. He was thankful for the advice, and off he went.

I breathed a sigh of relief and called my friend to reassure them I was all right. In the end nothing happened, but I'd rather live by the rule "better safe than sorry" than experience the alternative. Besides, I didn't lie to the guy, it's a great trail! It still saddens me that you can never truly know who to trust, but I'm glad I know to be aware and cautious of my surroundings.

Relieved and left to my own devices, I got to work and captured the sunrise image, exactly as I had envisioned it. I packed up and headed back to town… and was surprised to find the entire town covered in fog! Crazy what difference a few miles can make. I actually captured one of my personal favorite images when I got back to town – a beautiful leafy green tree peeking out of the fog next to a country road. I am a sucker for trees and fog!

Altogether, I was safe and it had been a highly successful day for a photography outing!

MY MOM'S ALL-TIME FAVORITE STORY

Grand Teton National Park | Wyoming, United States

EXPOSURE
Shutter 1/1000 sec. | Aperture f/4.5 | ISO 1250

CAMERA GEAR
Nikon D610 | Nikkor 200-400 f/4.0 | Shot @ 400mm

september 2014

My photography career has had two chapters so far. The first was learning through high school and college, plus my first attempt at making a living at photography when I moved home to Rapid City in 2003. Sadly about a zillion other photographers had already set up shop in my home town, and the eventual slump in the economy made it unlikely I'd make a living doing photography. So I went back to school, got a business degree, and worked in other fields for a while.

But I couldn't deny my passion for photography, and it was nagging at me to dive back in. So in 2014, I made the decision to try again. Needing to build up my portfolio, I asked my mom to join me on an adventure to a photographic favorite, Yellowstone National Park.

At the time I was lucky enough to have friends who lived in the park, and we were able to stay with them for our first week. It turned out to be a particularly great time for wildlife at Mammoth Hot Springs, where we were staying. It was rutting season for the elk and they surrounded the house! I loved the shooting opportunity, and my mom loved being surrounded by the majestic animals.

After that enjoyable stay, we decided to spend a few nights at the Old Faithful Lodge, something neither of us had done before. We didn't stay in the historic part of the hotel, but it was still lovely and it was so great to be able to wake up right next to Old Faithful. We even had a window facing the geyser! It was an unforgettable stay, and the trip was just getting better and better.

On our last morning in Yellowstone before heading down to Grand Teton National Park, my mom slept in while I got up to look for wildlife one last time. I was hoping to find some bison by the Grand Prismatic Pool to get a shot with all the steam, but instead I was treated to something else: my first ever wolf sighting!

I was on the road heading north, just past the Fountain Paint Pots when I saw three animals – black, white and grey – cross the field past the Paint Pots. At first I didn't even know what I was looking at, and wolves were so unexpected that I almost didn't believe my eyes. Wolves have been in the park since they were reintroduced in 1995, but they're elusive creatures and a sighting is rare.

Like mother, like daughter!

Since they were far away and running, my pictures of that sighting are nothing to write home about. I was sad that I'd have to go tell my mom what she'd missed. She'd been hoping we'd get to see a wolf.

She was a bit disappointed of course, but being the positive person that she is, she took it as a sign that we might see more. I was doubtful.

We packed up and headed south. After passing Grant Village, my mom asked me why I didn't think we'd see any more wolves. Having researched the wolves a bit, I told her they were mostly

Reflections of the Day Surprise wolf sighting driving from Yellowstone to the Tetons – Yellowstone National Park, USA   September 2014

seen in the Hayden and Lamar areas, opposite from the direction we were going. Heck, I was amazed I'd seen them earlier in the day! I told her our chances of seeing a wolf were slim at best.

At this point we came upon some backed up vehicles. Usually this means someone spotted wildlife, but I couldn't see anything. All of a sudden my mom pointed out the window and said, "Well, then what's that?"

I lifted up and leaned to look at where she was pointing, and whaddya know, it was a wolf! The road dropped off to a small pond and there he was, casually having a drink.

I wish I'd been more prepared for quick road-side shooting! I hurried to get out of the car and grab my camera, and scrambled with my exposures to get a good, sharp picture. I was so focused on the exposure that I didn't even flip the camera to do a vertical shot, and I almost missed the reflection in the water!

The photo is grainer than I'd like, and I really wish I'd gotten that vertical shot… but this is one of those images that outshines others because of the memories it holds. Now, I just smile every time my mom retells her favorite story.

AREN'T PARKS SUPPOSED TO BE PEACEFUL?

Grand Teton National Park | Wyoming, United States

EXPOSURE
Shutter 1/3 sec. | Aperture f/18 | ISO 400

CAMERA GEAR
Nikon D610 | Nikkor 70-200 f/4.0 | Shot @ 125mm

october 2014

When going to the Tetons for photography, anyone who is anyone has heard of Oxbow Bend, where this image was taken. In October of 2014 I set off on a planned trip with my Mom to catch the fall colors in the Tetons because we'd missed them in 2004. Sadly, before we had even left, I knew from posts on Facebook that we would miss the fall colors yet again. It's hard to predict when the leaves will change in the mountains.

I tried to not let this knowledge get me down though, and I told myself there would be many other stories to capture with my camera. This is one of those stories! This trip had a few WTF moments.

We started our trip a week before this image was created and explored Yellowstone National Park. Thankfully our week in Yellowstone turned into photography heaven with lovely moody mornings filled with fog. But after six straight mornings of nothing but fog, I was starting to crave a sunrise. I mean, all of my images were starting to look the same. So, day after day, I got up early hoping for some warm golden rays.

I actually had a morning when I went to Lower Falls in Yellowstone and it looked like I might get a sunrise! But when I arrived at my spot it was already filled with 15 other photographers (take note of that number for later). I tried to set up and frame a shot, but I wasn't finding it with the crowd and gave up after a few failed attempts. I figured the clear skies would hold out and I could try again tomorrow.

But then came a full week of never-ending "atmospheric haze," as photographer Tom Murphy would call it. Don't get me wrong, I LOVE fog, but I'd had my fill of it this trip and was ready for some sunshine! Needless to say, at this point I was starting to regret bailing on the Lower Falls sunrise so quickly.

We were stationed in the Mammoth area for the first half of the trip and then moved to the Old Faithful area to photograph sunrises, sunsets and stars. But AGAIN, we were all fogged in. I was still able to create some great shots, but none that included the elusive sun. However, I still had some travelling left, so I kept my hopes up.

Next up on our trip was the Tetons, where I prayed the sun would show itself. We seemed to have tidings of good luck when driving to the Tetons, as we had the luckiest chance meeting I have ever had with an animal along the way. This encounter deserves it's own story, and you can read about it in **my mom's favorite story, previous page**.

As we continued on to the Tetons, the skies seemed a bit more clear and it looked like I was finally going to luck out and get a sunrise the next morning. Since it was October, I thought for sure I would have a bit more peace and quiet down here. Boy, was I ever wrong.

Before bed that night I got everything ready, setting the alarm for 5:30 am since I only had to drive five minutes for my shot location. When the alarm went off (after what felt like only five minutes of sleep), I quickly turned it off so I wouldn't wake my mom, and I dragged myself out of bed. I won't lie – after a week of getting up early I was exhausted, but I bundled up and headed out the door.

Apparently I was not the only person missing the sun. As I rounded the corner near Oxbow Bend, I saw headlights and flashlights… and the closer I got the more evident it became that I would not be alone for sunrise.

In fact, I would estimate that there were upwards of 150 photographers already set-up and ready to catch the sunrise! I was shocked. I was suddenly wishing I had appreciated that moment at Lower Falls when only 15 photographers surrounded me. (Imagine me smacking my forehead here.)

I felt discouraged at the sight of the crowd, but pushed forward with my plan. I was determined not to miss this

Frosted in Pink Oxbow Bend: my multi-image panoramic... no people allowed! – Grand Teton National Park, USA   October 2014

sunrise! I parked the car, grabbed my bag and defiantly starting walking AWAY from everyone. I had to find a spot that I could call my own. While walking I thought to myself, "I must make it different." With so many of us, I had to somehow make my image stand out.

I concluded that most photographers in the crowd would be shooting normal rectangular shots, so I was going to focus the majority of my composition time on a panoramic layout. I finally located a spot where not only was I away from everyone, but I was even out of sight, hidden from the main group! Ha, privacy at last!

I focused on getting my gear ready to finally capture a sunrise. Just as I finished setting my exposure, I heard twigs snapping and leaves crunching. Apparently MY spot also looked to be a great spot for Mr. Nosey John Doe to set-up his gear as well. I won't lie, I had to try very hard to not give him the stink eye, but I was really bummed. And then he plopped his stuff… right… next… to MINE!

Really dude?

A few minutes later I noticed another guy had showed up above me. Where were they all coming from?! At some point I had to let my disappointment go so I could focus on the task at hand. The sun was just starting her display and pink began to frost the mountains. Finally!

I just loved how moody the sky was behind the peaks for this shot, and I could not wait to see how this sunrise panned out (ha ha ha, get it, panned, panoramic… oh come on, I know you're laughing with me).

Just as I finished snapping the three images that were used to create the panoramic above, the sun moved behind a cloud and the show was over. That was all she wrote! My first sunrise in almost a week and she lasted a whole whopping ten minutes.

Don't get me wrong - I love the image that came of that morning, but I will never stop wondering what might have been had she been allowed to fully rise to meet the mountains. And if I didn't have annoying people invading my hidden spot. Boooo!

WELL THAT WAS UNEXPECTED

Grand Teton National Park | Wyoming, United States

EXPOSURE
Shutter 57 sec. | Aperture f/22 | ISO 100

CAMERA GEAR
Nikon D610 | Nikkor 17-35 f/2.8 | Shot @ 25mm

october 2014

When my mom and I took off on a road trip to explore Yellowstone and Grand Teton National Parks in the fall of 2014, we hadn't travelled together since 2007. A much needed mother-daughter girl's trip was long overdue! My mom is one of the people who enjoys going on photography trips with me, so I brought my gear with the goal of capturing amazing, golden, sunny fall photos, and my mom was there just to relax and take it all in.

On that trip, our days typically went like this: I'd get up early to explore and try for a sunrise shot, then I'd head back to the hotel and spend the day with mom; later I'd head out alone to find a sunset shot, and I'd come back in the evening to collapse into bed while mom enjoyed a good book.

Despite my dogged efforts to capture sunrises and sunsets, most of my mornings and evenings were lacking in stunning color. During the entire trip, I ended up with just one good sunrise and one good sunset to shoot. But I got them! Both images are still some of my favorites, even after several years. (Wow, time sure ticks by fast…)

This image was one of the rewards for my efforts. It had been overcast and cruddy most of the day, but I thought I could ~just~ see a gap in the clouds behind the peaks. It was our last day and years ago in Glacier I had already learned my lesson about possibly missing something amazing **(see the "When in Doubt, Get Up and Go" story on page 35)**, so I still headed out to shoot. And hey, even if nothing epic happens with stunning color, there is always still something beautiful to see.

I left my mom at our hotel as I rushed off to catch what I thought would be a dud sunset. I had already scoped out a spot earlier, so I knew right where to go and set up my tripod. I pulled into the lot and was excited to see I was the only one there! And not only that, but I was rewarded with one of the most beautiful sunsets I've ever seen as the golden light suddenly came crashing through the clouds.

It looked as if the doors to heaven had been left open and holy light was shining down onto the earth.

Watching these moments alone in the peace and tranquility of nature is one of my favorite things about what I do. Each experience is truly special. Being able to witness such breathtaking beauty and know that this moment in time belongs solely to me… moments like these are the memories I will hold on to and treasure forever.

Just as the light was turning to the stunning pink shade I absolutely love, my moment was intruded upon. A car came screeeeeeeching into the parking lot, doors slamming with literal shouts of "We made it!" and "Oh wow, we got here just in time!" The sound of thundering feet came crashing down the path, and a group of teens took up residence just 30 feet away.

You'd think that'd be it, right? You'd think they'd be far enough away for us all to enjoy nature's beauty in peace, right? Not so much. My mood went from tranquil to annoyed as they kept up a continuous LOUD chatter the entire time.

So this story encompasses two "What the f?" moments: one of absolute awe at nature's beauty… and one of utter disappointment at the inconsiderate intrusion. I try to hold on to that awe when I look at this image, but it still, to this day, turns sour at the thought of those kids.

I guess I'm getting old or something! But for the sake of the world – please please PLEASE – if you're out in nature, have a little respect for peace and tranquility, and don't throw off someone's groove!

The Fiery Heavens Above Heavenly sunset light at Jenny Lake – Grand Teton National Park, USA

The Expanse of Time Old Faithful glowing in moonlight and accented by a star studded sky – Yellowstone National Park, USA

October 2014

GEYSERS AREN'T AFRAID OF THE DARK

Yellowstone National Park | Wyoming, United States

EXPOSURE
Shutter 30 sec. | Aperture f/4 | ISO 800

CAMERA GEAR
Nikon D610 | Nikkor 17-35 f/2.8 | Shot @ 17mm

october 2014

When I take on a new art project, I am ALL IN. I research how to do it, what supplies or equipment I need, the best way to do it, and I am ready to go. As in, right away! Let's do it NOW!

There has been, however, one exception to this trend: astrophotography.

Why, you ask? Well, I'm just going to come out and say it… I am afraid of the dark. Yep! I have been ever since I was a child. I mean, don't get me wrong, it's not as bad now as when I was little. But still, I'm not a fan - and if you look at the details of this story's images, you'll notice the STARS in the sky. So little 'ol me, afraid of the dark, braved the nighttime not once but TWICE to try out this new photography trend.

I'd done the research and was ready to try it long before these photos were taken, but you need to be away from city lights for night sky shots, and that was the hold-up. I was totally OK heading out on a sunset shoot by myself where I could quickly pack up and leave when it got dark. I was NOT OK with the idea of going out in the wild when it's pitch black outside.

But in 2014, opportunity knocked! I was heading out on a road trip to the greater Yellowstone area with my mom, and a number of things were lining up to let me try nighttime shooting. We were staying at the inn right next to Old Faithful, presenting a nice safe subject not too far into the wild, and the fall-time quarter-moon meant I'd have enough light to expose the geyser and foreground, but not so much that it would block out the stars. Plus, Old Faithful is, well… faithful!

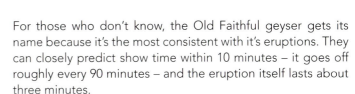

▲ Mom & I bundled up on a chilly day at geyser central!

For those who don't know, the Old Faithful geyser gets its name because it's the most consistent with it's eruptions. They can closely predict show time within 10 minutes – it goes off roughly every 90 minutes – and the eruption itself lasts about three minutes.

Three minutes really isn't sufficient time to get your shot, especially when you're doing 30 second exposures on a tripod and operating your camera's buttons and dials in limited light.

I'd shot the geyser earlier that day and decided I liked a vertical shot, so I felt pretty prepared when I headed out for the first full-dark eruption at 8:30 pm. Soon after the eruption started, I realized I hadn't thought of something. The longer nighttime exposure means the camera picks up more of the geyser water getting blown sideways. Even with just a gentle breeze, my vertical composition was cutting off most of the geyser. Dang.

Back inside I went to wait 90 minutes, and then back outside for take two. I was surprised that I wasn't the only one out and about at 10pm! It was nice to see some tourists doing things against the grain. Perhaps they were out to see the stars as well, and good thing - we all got lucky as we were surprised by a star explosion!

Not sure if that's what you call it, but we all saw it. It was right in line with where we all gazed, waiting for Old Faithful to go off. A star all of a sudden went super, super bright and then POOF, it disappeared! So crazy. I wondered how long ago the star actually went out for the light to reach us at that moment, and what happened out there in the vastness of space that caused it to go out? It's humbling witnessing something like that and realizing just how big the universe is. Sigh… back to the task at hand! I set up for a horizontal composition this time, and as wide as I could go with my lens. When the geyser went off, I could tell the eruption wasn't as powerful as the last time, but it turned out to be a good thing as all the steam fit in my frame. I ended up loving the composition and the feel of the stars in the sky. What a magical night. I realized that just because the sun sets, it doesn't mean the world falls asleep. There's so much to see, a world of wonder!

I was so pumped with my experience that when I saw that Castle Geyser was scheduled to go off around 10 pm the next night, I decided I'd go out again. I figured since I'd enjoyed shooting so much that I hadn't even cared it was dark the night before, then heck, maybe I'd outgrown my fear of the dark.

Yeah… not so much. My mom wasn't too keen on me taking off down the path, out of site, late at night… but I was still staying positive. I'm an adult, right? I got this! I have a flashlight!

So off I went, thinking "This isn't too bad, I can still see the lights of the lodge, it's all good!" And I kept that positive attitude as I reached Castle Geyser, trying to keep myself occupied by scoping out angles and setting up my gear.

But here's the thing – Castle Geyser is quite a bit further out from the lodge than Old Faithful, and the eruption timing is not as predictable. Castle Geyser often goes off either early or late by up to 45 minutes, and it only erupts every 10-12 hours, so I only had one chance! But the eruptions last 20 minutes, which is helpful. I got there early, and once I got my gear set up I had quite a bit of time to hang out and wait. By myself. In the dark. No comforting lodge just a few feet away… and this time, I was quite a bit closer to the wild!

Of course, at this point my brain starts pulling up all sorts of helpful information… such as how all the Yellowstone critters like bison, elk and bears, do NOT like to be surprised in the dark of night. And oh yeah, I remembered a grizzly had been spotted in the area earlier. Awesome!

So I did what any sane person would do. I started talking to myself VERY loudly, making sure the animals could hear me. I made it known that I did not want them eating me while I waited an hour or so to take my picture, thank you very much.

And as if that's not enough to set off my nerves, I noticed strange people walking towards me. Not near the lodge like the night before, but out in the FULL DARK. Don't get me wrong – the likelihood of these being crazy people was slim, but hey, I've read enough about murders in forests to be a little bit worried at least. I mean, how many tourists watch geysers erupt at night?

Of course, they happened to be just that – tourists walking out to see the geyser erupt at night, and tourists with great timing too! As soon as they arrived, off she went!

It had been so eerily quiet, and now suddenly the sound was like standing next to a 747 jet engine! Even though it was dark, the moon lit up the white steam beautifully. I got to work shooting, exposing for the stars and the light of the moon, which gave me this interesting image of Castle Geyser that mixes night and day - plus I captured a rainbow in the mist to boot! It was such a magnificent sight to see that even though I got my photo early on, I ended up shooting the entire eruption until the end. It was such a unique experience.

And I'd once again braved the night! But… I wasn't planning on making this a habit. I don't want to push my luck!

When I got back to my room, I told my mom that I wished she could have experienced that amazing show of nature with me. She was just glad I hadn't been eaten by a bear.

It's all about perspective, I suppose!

▲ Dramatic steamy water pouring into the river near Castle Geyser

From tourists to elk, YNP days get crowded! ▶

Elemental Dance Castle Geyser's powerful blast of water can even make a rainbow at night – Yellowstone National Park, USA

EXPOSURE Shutter 30 sec. | Aperture f/4.5 | ISO 1600 **CAMERA GEAR** Nikon D610 | Nikkor 17-35 f/2.8 | Shot @ 32mm

TEMPERAMENTAL ICE

Spearfish Canyon, The Black Hills | South Dakota, United States

EXPOSURE
Shutter 8 sec. | Aperture f/22 | ISO 100

CAMERA GEAR
Nikon D610 | Nikkor 17-35 f/2.8 | Shot @ 17mm

january 2015

This story has two What the f? moments. Two very, very different What the f? moments.

I have lived in Rapid City, South Dakota, basically my whole life, minus a few years away at college. So imagine my surprise when, in January of 2015 at the tender age of 33, I saw the Facebook feed for the local photo club fill up with pictures of an amazing ice cave I'd never seen! Apparently it was less than an hour away in Spearfish Canyon. How had I never seen this before?!?!

After much questioning I was told the spot is called Community Caves by the locals, and that it's one of those spots someone had to tell you about and you could only find with clues like "it's the little pull-off on the right after the third curve." There wouldn't be any signs to find this spot! I'd been led astray by someone's "directions" before, so I turned to the trusty Internet for specifics. I'm still not sure it's a good thing you can find these hidden spots online (then they get overrun), but on this day I was grateful.

I called up my usual partner in crime, my best friend Toni, and we planned a day to scour the canyon, seeking this mystery ice cave. We ended up picking the coldest day of the month! But we didn't let that deter us from setting off on this adventure to see something new in our back yard. We had layers, we had gear, we had directions – what could go wrong?

We merrily drove into Spearfish Canyon, excited to find this new gem among all the other sites we knew in the canyon. We passed Bridal Veil Falls. We passed the trailhead for Devil's Bathtub… huh. Shouldn't we have found it by now? When we reached the lodge and turn-off for Roughlock Falls, we knew we'd missed it somewhere along the way. Shoot.

▲ Massive ice flows at Community Caves

Since we were already that far in, we decided to stop at Eleventh Hour Gulch on the way back to check out the popular ice climbing spot. We went up pretty far and it was fun, but not what I was looking for photography-wise. On the way out we saw an ice climber setting up. "Hey!" Toni said, "I bet he knows where to find Community Caves!" So we asked him and sure enough, he knew… and it was all the way back at the start of the canyon.

And if that isn't funny enough, the guy was from Wyoming. So here we were, two local gals getting directions from the out-of-towner! We headed out and drove the almost 10 miles back to the start of the canyon and smacked our foreheads when we turned around and spotted the icy caves almost immediately. Sigh… well, at least we were warmed up!

The hike immediately put our gear to the test. After crossing an iced-over creek, the trail started uphill and got steep, fast – and remember, we're hiking on ICE! We could see long streaks where hapless hikers had taken on the climb without spikes and ended up sliding. I would NOT recommend taking on this hike without one-inch spikes and sturdy poles!

Being our first time to Community Caves, we had no idea what to expect. On the climb, I could tell the pictures I'd seen didn't do justice to the size and scale of this place. Reaching the top and stepping under the massive overhang to be enclosed in thick ice spires had us in AWE. It was such an unreal feeling, being surrounded by all these wondrous ice sculptures shaped simply by the dripping water we could hear echoing off the rock walls. It was stunningly beautiful. I had never seen anything like it in my life.

As I started to explore the ice flows, I was grateful for the new winter gear I'd invested in to prepare for an upcoming winter trip to Yellowstone. Heck, I was actually laying on the ice to get this shot and the cold didn't bother me one bit!

N-Ice to Know You The icy fangs of Community Caves, a treat for ice climbers and photographers alike! – Black Hills National Forest of South Dakota, USA

January 2015

But my friend was not so lucky – she'd had no reason to invest in heavy duty gear, and the cold was seeping through her budget snowboots and double layer of socks. She held out pretty long, but eventually had to say something. I felt bad for not noticing her discomfort, but I was so blown away by what I was seeing that it overrode any cold I was feeling.

I'll never forget that first time in the magical frozen wonderland of Community Caves. It was so impressive that when, exactly one year later, a friend from the local photography club who was impressed by my N-Ice To Know You image asked me to take him to the caves, I said, "Sure! Why not?"

I should have given the idea a little more consideration. You'll see a common theme in my stories of me planning ahead as much as possible to be prepared for a shoot, from researching gear to scoping out a location. But I'd never really had to think about being prepared to handle a situation with people until my January 2016 venture to Community Caves. What I should have taken into consideration is that the friend who wanted to go was an elderly gentleman. We'd gone to the Badlands together on a shoot before, and I'd remembered the loose, rocky terrain had been a bit tough to hike, but he'd done OK. He's normally very active… but still, I was a bit concerned about the steep, icy uphill hike to Community Caves.

I gave him the benefit of the doubt, however, and we planned our day to start with a sunrise shoot at a rustic barn by Bear Butte before heading to Spearfish Canyon about 30 miles away. I'd advised him on what gear would be needed to safely hike the ice in the canyon, and my concern kicked in again when we parked in the canyon and I saw he didn't have proper ice cleats. He assured me he would be fine so we set out.

As expected, the trail was solid ice and packed down from former hikers; Community Caves is one of the most popular winter treks in the canyon. And to make matters worse, it turned out my friend's hiking poles were also not up to the task and just wouldn't grip the ice.

Needless to say it was a stressful hike up, and I just didn't feel it was my place to call anything off as the "youngster" of the pair. Thankfully, we finally made it to the top, and I was relieved to reach a somewhat level area.

The cave was AWESOME. It was like walking into a giant icy mouth, totally different than the year before. That's what's so incredible about this location – it's always changing, depending on where the water flows and freezes. The flow is largely determined by Mother Nature, but also with the help of some avid ice climbers who direct the water by laying hoses up above.

We started exploring the cave, finding compositions that interested us. After about 20 minutes I happened to notice that my friend had slipped, but he recovered quickly. I did another shot with my camera, and when I looked back over he was now sitting down and eating a sandwich. I decided to go over and just ask if he was feeling OK. He said he was feeling tired and thought he should eat. He didn't quite seem totally "with it" though, so I kept asking him questions.

As I was talking, he just… laid back on the ice and started moving weird, going side to side. This was not right. I was instantly on my feet, hovering over him and yelling his name. My mind was in a panic. All I could think was, "His wife is going to kill me!"

My brain held on to this not-helpful thought as I stood over my friend, screaming his name with no response.

I was at a loss, tears streaming down my face… and my brain finally kicked in to action mode. I needed to

▲ Scrambling up into Eleventh Hour Gulch

Keeping warm in good gear outside of Community Caves ▶

◀ Icy pools peek through mounds of snow on the Devils Bathtub hike.

EXPOSURE Shutter 0.8 sec. | Aperture f/22 | ISO 100   **CAMERA GEAR** Nikon D810 | Nikkor 17-35 f/2.8 | Shot @ 17mm

Frozen Fangs The icy fangs of Community Caves in Spearfish Canyon – Black Hills National Forest of South Dakota, USA   January 2016

get help, NOW. I moved his camera bag and tried to get him as secure as possible. I was going to have to leave him. To get to cell service, I'd have to scramble all the way back down the icy hill, get to the car and drive towards town until I got a signal. The trek normally takes at least 15 minutes, and I didn't know how far I'd have to drive… How would I get him help in time?!?

All of this flew through my head in a matter of seconds. Just as I was about to take my first step to race for help… he sat up. He looked at me and asked what was wrong.

I was in shock. He had no idea that anything had just happened. He didn't even know he'd been laying down.

It turned out that he'd had an episode like this once before and had been put on medication, but he'd forgotten to take his dose that morning. I swore after that I'd be more prepared. Anything can happen out in the wilderness, away from help, whether it's up a mountain or right next to the road.

I enrolled in classes and am now a certified Wilderness First Responder. I keep up with the renewal process so that I can confidently handle situations like this.

To find out more about the **Wilderness First Responder** program, Google the term and find the organization closest to you. I went to **www.nols.edu**.

Protein Snack Hungry little bluebird getting its fill – Custer State Park of South Dakota, USA

June 2015

ODDLY SATISFYING

Custer State Park | South Dakota, United States

EXPOSURE
Shutter 1/640 sec. | Aperture f/4 | ISO 400

CAMERA GEAR
Nikon D610 | Nikkor 200-400 f/4 .0 | Shot @ 400mm

2015 June

One of the best things to do when purchasing a new lens is to first rent it to test it out. Lenses are like cars – a pricey investment – nowhere near as costly as a new car, but comparable to some used cars – and they lose value immediately. It's not cheap to rent a lens, but a few hundred dollars to rent can keep you from losing a grand or more later on if the lens ends up not fitting your needs.

I hadn't quite figured this out in 2015, and I had excitedly traded in one of my lenses to help me purchase a monster zoom lens. You know the ones – you see photographers using them in parks and the lens is so big it needs its own tripod! I was excited to be THAT photographer.

I decided to first use it shooting the colorful little birds that inhabit Custer State Park's "Bird Box Row," as local bird-watching enthusiasts call it. The park is a haven for birdwatchers, with bird lookouts everywhere – the park provides special bird houses for the winged critters to use when nesting and having babies, and the birds also love to perch on posts distributed throughout the park. The park rangers also host special bird-watching events and have classes to teach you how to build a bird box. (And no, it's not just a shoe box with holes in it!)

I had a lens to test though, so I skipped the ranger events and headed out to Bird Box Row by myself. I picked a spot among the lookouts and carefully set up my gear, doing my best not to disturb the birdies. I perched (ha ha!) behind my camera and stood very still, settling in to let the birds get used to me in the hopes they'd go about their normal daily business. I spent at least an hour watching and photographing all the birds. So peaceful and pretty!

The best part was when the mama and papa birds flew in to feed the babies and you could hear the young'uns chirping away. The parents seemed to like landing in the same spots each time, and that helped me focus in on a landing zone and be ready to capture my shot in advance.

I worked so fast that I didn't notice any particulars about the birds, concentrating mainly on whether or not I had them in focus. So when I got home and zoomed in on my shots, I was like, "What's that in your mouth?" I was surprised to see a wide variety of bugs in their beaks! I mean, of course they're eating bugs, but I didn't expect to be able to count their legs and ID the bug.

I especially loved this shot where the bird has a dead spider in its clutches. I hate spiders. Good birdie!

So what about the lens? Though it worked out great for the birds, when I tried it out on wildlife further away, the images were soft. Ugh. I lost a lot of cash value when I tried to re-sell the lens, and belatedly realized I'd have been better off just renting the behemoth.

And hey, it's FUN to rent a lens and try it out!

Had It Up To Here Ponderosa pines get their feet wet in flooded Pactola Reservoir – Black Hills National Forest of South Dakota, USA

June 2015

ALWAYS DOUBLE CHECK

Pactola Reservoir in the Black Hills | South Dakota, United States

EXPOSURE
Shutter 13 sec. | Aperture f/6.3 | ISO 400

CAMERA GEAR
Nikon D610 | Nikkor 70-200 f/4.0 | Shot @ 82mm

2015 june

At the time this image was created, I was working part-time at the South Dakota State Railroad Museum and travelling back and forth between Rapid City and Hill City, where the 1880 Train and the museum were located. Of course, the photographer in me is always on the lookout for an exciting photo opp, and I would take different routes through the Black Hills on the way to and from work, hoping to find inspiration.

June of 2015 ended up providing some very unique views in the hills, as we had heavy rains after years of drought. Drought usually means the ground is too dry to soak up an influx of water quickly, so all the area lakes and creeks were flooded. I was particularly awed by Pactola Reservoir, one of our biggest and most popular lakes, as it looked to be (I'm guessing) 20 feet higher than normal! Marinas and beaches were covered and the side roads to the best spots were partially closed due to the high water.

I could see these trees from the highway and was shocked to see them submerged so far in the water. This is normally a popular picnic spot. I just had to get a shot of this unusual sight and knew the water levels could drop any time. Fortunately, I soon had a day where I could leave work early enough to catch evening and sunset light!

All was going to plan. The sky had clouds that would be lovely during golden hour, and I was plenty early. I had to park and hike into the spot, so I'd been sure to leave work promptly to give myself time to explore. I parked, popped the hatch on my little car and started collecting my gear... and that's when I realized that I was missing my card case with ALL of my cards. There wasn't even a card in the camera.

I grumbled to myself as I shut the hatch and got back in my car to rush home. "I am such an idiot!"

I raced back to my house, some 20 minutes away, and ran inside to get the cards. I looked in my desk where I normally store them… and they weren't there. What the f???

I looked everywhere, and NO case. Nothing. Nada.

I stopped and thought… wait… could it be? Nah…

I went back out to the car and yep, they were in there the whole time, tucked in my bag. Insert eye roll, forehead slap and cuss words. Ugh.

I thankfully made it back to Pactola and had time to hike in and get this photo, grateful that an interesting sunset provided unique light that perfectly fit the setting.

The lessons learned? Always double check, and get to your spot early. Very, very, very early!

The Majestic Mr. Billy He's king of the world! Well, of this mountain, at least... — Glacier National Park, USA

July 2015

PLEASE DON'T GORE ME...

Glacier National Park | Montana, United States

EXPOSURE
Shutter 1/640 sec. | Aperture f/4 | ISO 400

CAMERA GEAR
Nikon D610 | Nikkor 70-200 f/4 | Shot @ 110mm

2015

A photography road trip in 2015 was the first time I was going to drive all the way to Banff and Jasper up in the Canadian Rockies, and I was happy to be able to plan a detour to Glacier National Park on the way.

I'd fallen in love with the (comparatively) little park when I first visited with my mom in 2007, enamored with everything from the bears and mountain goats to the lakes and snow covered peaks. So in 2015, I planned to hit the west side of the park on the way up, and the east side on the way back down. Why go once when you can go twice, right?

Glacier is, of course, packed with tourists in the middle of July, and since forest fires wrecked my chances of sunrise and sunset pictures on this trip, I frequently ended up where the crowds were. It started early on when I headed out to explore the Hidden Lake Overlook and found my first group of tourists. There wasn't much to "look over" in the smoke, but luckily the goats were out in full force that day!

There were so many mountain goats along the trail, babies included, that you had to be careful not to get caught in between them. They may look harmless, but they're still wild animals and personally, I'd rather not get gored!

They drew a crowd, of course, and as all us tour-ons (yep, I admit it, I was one of them that day) started to get a little too close, the goats got annoyed and were zigging and zagging every which direction.

One particular billy was quite majestic, lounging on a ledge overlooking his domain… and apparently getting irritated with all the commotion. He suddenly decided to get up, and there was no other direction for him to go except right towards our group of onlookers. Trust me, up close these goats are bigger than they seem!

I started backing away, but some tourists were really pushing their luck. One guy had sauntered within 10 feet of the big boss goat, shooting video and going on about how he was getting back to nature or something. (If I was the goat, I would be irritated too.) Another tourist didn't bother moving until he was close enough to touch the goat.

Heck, I'd pushed the boundaries climbing up the cliffs a bit to get my shot, but I wasn't THAT close! I was plenty happy with how close I could shoot with my zoom lens.

> "Let's all set better examples for future generations."

I then actually caught myself hiding behind another tourist while all of this drama was going on. The older gentleman that I was using as a shield assured me we were fine where we were, but still… I wasn't taking any chances, and I didn't want to perturb the goat any more than we already had.

That poor billy was being pushed to his limits, and I certainly didn't want to be the last straw!

The point of this story is that sometimes we need to override our heart's desires and do what's respectful. For photographers, it's more important to give Mother Nature the respect she deserves than to overstep the line in pursuit of a great shot.

As tourists, we all need to realize that nature is just as enjoyable when viewed from a safe distance. Let's all set better examples for future generations. And remember to pack a zoom lens, or at least some binoculars!

THE UN-HEARTBREAK HOTEL

Banff National Park | Alberta, Canada

EXPOSURE
Shutter 1.6 sec. | Aperture f/8 | ISO 400

CAMERA GEAR
Nikon D610 | Nikkor 17-35 f/2.8 | Shot @ 26mm

2015 july

As you may have read before, my first trip to the Canadian Rockies was in 2014 with my best friend, Toni. We flew into Calgary on that trip and rented a car that we would drive north and drop off in Edmonton where we'd fly out. We stuck pretty close to our budget that trip, but one unexpected cost was the park pass. We found out when entering the park that since we'd be going through multiple national parks, it would be cheaper to buy an annual all-park pass.

Driving away from the park gate, Toni joked, "You know what that means, right? We have to come back within a year so our pass doesn't go to waste!" We laughed it off – neither of us could afford the plane tickets and car rental again.

When winter rolled around that year, I peeked at the pricing for hotels… and they were so much cheaper! Hmmm… I looked up how long it would take to drive to Banff from the Black Hills. 15 hours?!?! That's doable! I called Toni and said, "Soooo… if the trip was affordable, would you really go back?" She pretty much said, "Duh." So I planned us a Canadian road trip for July of 2015!

But it wasn't meant to be for Toni. My best friend has an autoimmune disease, and in February of 2015 she had one of the worst episodes she'd ever had and ended up in the ER. One life flight later and my friend was at Mayo Clinic where she opted to have major surgery. She ended up in and out of the hospital for months, and recovery was slow.

Everything was booked for our epic besties road trip… but I'd be going alone.

▲ Where's Erica??? Yes, I'm in this 2014 picture at Bow Glacier Falls!

It was heartbreaking to me – she has been one of the most amazing friends anyone could ask for and it sucked to leave her behind. She told me, "Hey, we'll just have to go again! And again!" (She fell in love with Banff as much as I did.) She sent me on my way with a promise to take a ton of great pictures for her. That, I can do!

On our first trip in 2014, we'd only had a day to explore the Icefields Parkway on the way to the Athabasca Glacier. We'd first pulled off at Bow Lake and gone into the lodge there to ask if there were any good hikes by the lake. The very nice people at the Num-Ti-Jah Lodge, as we learned it was called, said we could hike behind the lake to Bow Glacier Falls, the source of the lake's glacial teal water. Excited, we took off!

It was a gorgeous hike and the falls were so impressive that we didn't mind how exhausted we were as we headed out to the next stop. The turn for Peyto Lake was just a few more minutes up the parkway. We discovered you can't see this lake from the road and have to hike straight uphill from the parking lot to get to the viewpoint. It was totally worth the jaunt, but the bright midday light didn't lend itself to photography.

So in 2015, I was determined to get an epic picture from the lookout over Peyto Lake.

Since Toni and I had been intrigued by the lodge at Bow Lake and it was close enough to get to Peyto Lake for the best light, I'd booked a few nights there. Now, this place had looked cool but I wasn't expecting too much from a rustic lodge that runs on its own generators. (I found out about the generators when the power went off the first night and I heard the staff cheering when they powered back up.) I was happily proven wrong about the pleasure of staying at this place! The Num-Ti-Jah is, to this day, one of

Wish You Were Here My epic but lonely sunset at Peyto Lake – Banff National Park, Canada

July 2015

my favorite places I've ever stayed. It's quaint and charming and, unlike a regular lodge, you eat at reserved times in their dining room each night, enjoying meals prepared by gourmet chefs. It was HEAVENLY… and it made me miss my friend even more.

But I missed her the most when I captured the sunset image at Peyto Lake. As I sat and watched the smoky sunset create amazing shades of purple and pink above the lush green forest and teal lake, I thought of how much she would have loved being there to enjoy the spectacle. I wished my photo buddy was with me.

My reflective moment was interrupted, unexpectedly, by mosquitos, of all things! I thought being so far north in glacial areas that the little critters wouldn't be so thick, but they were horrible!

Regardless of the pests, I still took the picture for Toni and titled it "Wish You Were Here" with her in mind. I surprised her with the title when I showcased it in a local photo exhibit, and she teared up a bit when we went to see it in the gallery.

Thankfully we did get to go back to the Canadian Rockies and enjoy these spots together! We did a trip in the fall of 2017 and I nabbed us a couple of nights at the Num-Ti-Jah before they closed for the season. To our pleasant surprise we caught their celebration of Canadian Thanksgiving and got to enjoy a big social meal in the dining room with all the guests and staff! Plus, we got to experience yellow-needled larch trees in fall and snowfall at glacial lakes for the first time.

And trust me, we'll be going back again.

Finally! Road trip besties at the Peyto Lake lookout in 2017, after hiking up in snow!

Below, frigid shooting conditions at wintery Bow Lake

The Num-Ti-Jah Lodge at the edge of Bow Lake, its cozy dining room and our horseshoe key, plus the famed red chairs found throughout Canadian National Parks

EXPOSURE Shutter 0.4 sec. | Aperture f/16 | ISO 64   **CAMERA GEAR** Nikon D810 | Nikkor 14-24 f/2.8 | Shot @ 16mm

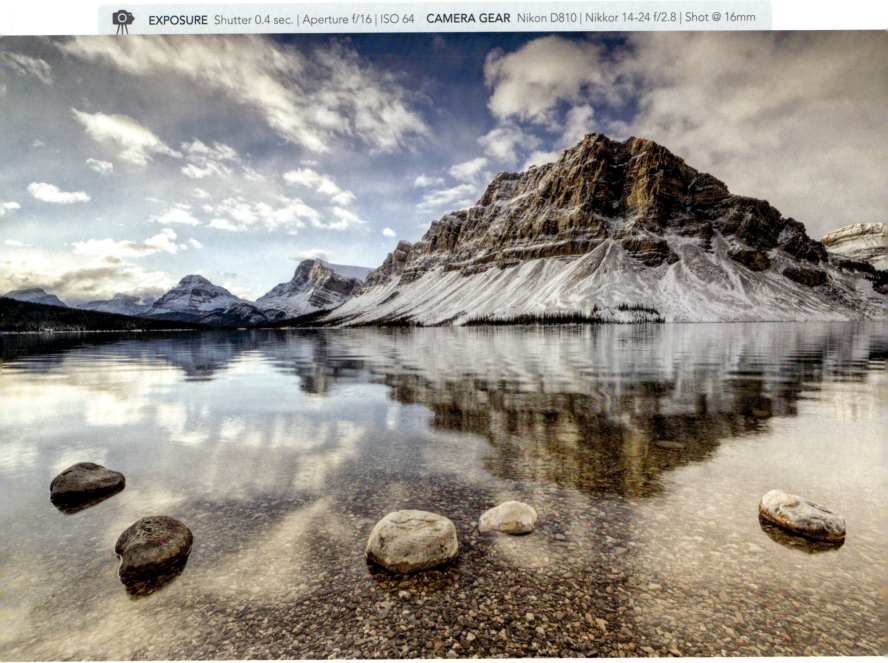

Golden Dreams Fall brings a different mix of light to Bow Lake – Banff National Park, Canada

October 2017

SPUR OF THE MOMENT

Jasper National Park | Alberta, Canada

EXPOSURE
Shutter 1/160 sec. | Aperture f/9 | ISO 400

CAMERA GEAR
Nikon D610 | Nikkor 17-35 f/2.8 | Shot @ 17mm

2015 July

On the last night of my 2015 stay in Jasper up in the Canadian Rocky Mountains, I thought I'd better do what all good tourists do and ride the tramway. I'd already ridden both the Banff and Lake Louise tramways, so I thought I'd go for the trifecta and finish out my set.

Let me just say that if you have to choose only one tramway while you're in the Canadian Rockies, the Jasper SkyTram is IT! It takes you so high above everything that it's a surreal experience to look down at the world – especially in my case with the passing of a majestic storm.

It had rained profusely that day, making it difficult to photograph the scenery. I'd pretty much hit all the spots I wanted to, except Maligne Canyon. This was the second time I wasn't able to properly photograph the area: the lake was overly crowded on my first trip, and this time a fire had cut off access to the road.

Frustrated from trying to access the canyon and failing, I decided I needed to do something fun for my last day. I figured the tram would be interesting even in the rain, so I headed that way. In the parking lot I thought I'd give the storm a little time to maybe pass by, and to my delight it did! I grabbed my gear, got my ticket and was soon on my way up the mountain.

It soon became evident that this tram was much different than the one in Banff. I was heading ABOVE the tree line! I watched the view open up before me, and when the sun snuck through and illuminated the scene, I could see the entirety of the storm still going strong a few miles off.

I stared out of the tram in awe at one of the most amazing scenes I'd ever seen. I was high above the storm, actually looking on a level at the middle of the storm… and looking DOWN at the ends of a complete rainbow arcing out of the thunderous cloud.

It was so stunning. I willed the tram to move faster – I needed to be taking pictures ASAP!

We arrived at the top and I quickly got to work trying to capture this unusual and breathtaking once-in-a-lifetime view. Fellow photographers, would you believe… my 17 mm wasn't wide enough! If only I'd had the 14-24 mm lens back then, perhaps I could've captured the full breadth of what my eyes were seeing! I made do though and captured this image to remember the moment.

I was treated to multiple views of rainbows while I explored the area and climbed to the very top of the mountain. Being up that high in the rocky tundra is such a treat! It almost feels like you're on another planet.

I shared the tram ride with a nice couple on the way down. They had actually HIKED up the mountain instead of riding the tram! What a climb. It turned out they'd parked elsewhere and hiked a ways before reaching the base of the mountain. They were ready to be done with walking for the day and asked if I would give them a ride to their car. On a whim, I said yes! They became my first hitchhikers.

I don't normally do this out of the common fear of getting mugged or something worse. Of course, that didn't happen – I'd trusted my instincts and knew these were decent people. They even tracked me down online later to again thank me for the ride.

It's nice to see that the world is not as awful as some would have you believe, and that some (cautious) spontaneity can be rewarded with rainbows and happy encounters with good human beings.

Above the Storm Looking down at a thunderhead from Whistler Mountain, top of the The Jasper SkyTram – Jasper National Park, Canada   July 2015

EXPLORE, SNOOZE, REPEAT

Glacier National Park | Montana, United States

EXPOSURE
Shutter 2.5 sec. | Aperture f/16 | ISO 400

CAMERA GEAR
Nikon D610 | Nikkor 17-35 f/2.8 | Shot @ 20mm

2015 July

If you've read any of my stories, you likely know by now that I'm a little obsessed with sunrises and sunsets. Other than wildlife, it's pretty much what I'm always planning my photo trips around. For the first part of my 2015 trip to Glacier, I'd been cheated out of either type of shot due to a forest fire. The thick smoke was hindering any chance of color.

So on the last night of my trip, I was DETERMINED! Nothing was going to stop me from getting some sort of sunset shot, other than a torrential downpour. I decided to drive up the well-known Going-to-the-Sun Road for a higher vantage point. I headed out from the Apgar Village around 3:30 pm to give myself plenty of time to explore.

The whole day had been rainy on and off, and I was hopeful that the spotty clouds would let some light through right at sunset time. But when I arrived to the Hidden Lake Overlook parking area, I was treated to the very torrential downpour I'd hoped to avoid. But it was early, I could still get lucky! I hunkered down in my car to wait out the storm. And I slept. Hey, what else was I going to do?

I woke up after an hour, and it was still raining cats and dogs. Defeated, I left and headed back down the mountain. Halfway down, the sun came out!!! I pulled over to get some shots, then turned around and raced back to the parking lot.

And it started raining again. Dag nab it! Well, I'd seen that the storm was spotty, I just needed to be patient. So I parked… and took another hour long nap. What can I say? Rainy weather makes me sleepy.

This time, waiting paid off and the rain let up. I jumped out to get pictures of a sudden rainbow, but I still had quite a bit of time until I needed to hike to the lookout for sunset. I decided to head further down the road and explore a bit. On the way down the other side of the mountain, I saw the strangest thing – a wave of fog was moving towards me, and it was moving FAST! I'd never seen fog move like that. I once again pulled over to photograph the unexpected view and got a few shots of the crazy phenomenon

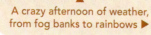

A crazy afternoon of weather, from fog banks to rainbows ▶

The Beauty of the Storm An elusive sunset captured from Hidden Lake Overlook – Glacier National Park, USA

July 2015

before I found myself engulfed in the fog. I thought, well, if I didn't get an epic sunset, at least I'd have some cool shots of fog!

But I was still determined to get that sunset. I headed back to the visitor center, packed up and headed out on the trail. Uphill hikes take me a while when I'm hauling 20+ pounds of gear, but I made it to the lookout in time. The rain had stopped for a spell, but the wind was horrendous! It was blowing continuously, blasting me in the face at 35-50 MPH. I did everything I could to weigh down my tripod so I could set a decent ISO and shutter. No point in putting in all this effort just to get a grainy or blurry photo. I managed to get everything secure enough for decent settings, and finally, after days and days of NO sunsets, I got this shot.

My composition is still not quite what I wanted (oh darn, guess I need to go back!), but the misadventures leading up to this moment make it one of my most memorable sunsets to date, and I remember my determination finally paying off. That's what makes art so special - the memories and emotions it evokes.

BISON JAMS AND FINDING GOLD

Yellowstone National Park | Wyoming, United States

EXPOSURE
Shutter 1/80 sec. | Aperture f/11 | ISO 800

CAMERA GEAR
Nikon D610 | Nikkor 70-200 f/4.0 | Shot @ 70mm

october 2015

Yellowstone National Park is one of my favorite places to go for a quick photo trip. In October of 2015 I headed over to the park for a week to unwind, and I was hoping for the same lovely weather pattern of rain and fog that I'd had on a visit the year before. Contrary to common belief, bright sunshine is not ideal for photographs as the light is too harsh. Softer light at sunrise or sunset is ideal – "Golden Hour" as it's called – but the right type of cloudy weather can give a photographer plenty of soft, dreamy light to play with.

To my dismay, 2015's weather did not look like it was going to deliver. I was greeted with clear blue skies, not a cloud in sight, and a balmy 60 degrees – a photographer's worst nightmare! Yes, most travelers hope for exactly this type of sunshiny day, but I was disappointed.

I spent most of the week catching up on sleep. Terrible, I know. The sunny weather was hindering my creative juices!

So I was grateful when one morning, I woke up to an overcast sky. Maybe I'd find some fog! I thought it was the perfect opportunity to head to Lamar to capture some wildlife shots. Inspired, I packed up The Blueberry (that's what we called my little blue car at the time – thanks Psych!) and headed out.

On the way, I passed a road called Blacktail Plateau Drive that I'd been down years ago. To my surprise, it was open, even though it was the start of the off season! "Let's do it!" I thought, feeling I was meant to take this route.

And then… a whole lot of nothing. Not much wildlife was about, and the cloud cover was getting too heavy for any good light. But then…

Here begins the series of BISON JAMS!

For those who don't know the term, a bison jam is when traffic gets held up due to the big creatures standing in the road. I first came across three bison, but they were still plenty big to make me cautious in my little Ford Fiesta. It took twenty minutes to get past them.

I was finally able to get out of the boring detour and back on the main road, but wouldn't you know it, there at the turn for Lamar Valley was another bison jam!

I was slowly making my way through this latest jam when all of a sudden, sunlight broke through and bam, there was a rainbow!

I quickly backed up into a spot ~mostly~ off the road and began to work fast. I fired off as many shots as I could, hoping one would be good. As most people know, bison are usually quite intent with their grass grazing. It's common for a photographer to get a ton of shots with their heads down where they end up looking like furry boulders!

As you can see from this image, I lucked out and in one frame I was able to capture a bison with his head up. The rainbow only lasted for maybe 10 minutes.

I just love thinking about how I would have missed it had it not been for the delay I experienced earlier. It's wonderful where life can lead us!

Good as Gold Close enough to a pot of gold, near Tower Junction – Yellowstone National Park, USA

October 2015

SO THAT'S WHAT FROSTBITE FEELS LIKE...

Badlands National Park | South Dakota, United States

EXPOSURE
Shutter 1.3 sec. | Aperture f/18 | ISO 200

CAMERA GEAR
Nikon D810 | Nikkor 17-35 f/2.8 | Shot @ 17mm

december 2015

Winter and I have not been the best of friends as I have grown older. I used to love playing in the snow when I was a kid, building forts and spending many hours out in the fluffy stuff. But I started to struggle with cold temperatures more and more as I got older, and in 2008, I was diagnosed with Raynaud's Disease. With Raynaud's, cold triggers my brain to send signals causing my blood vessels to constrict in an attempt to pull that warm blood to more vital organs. This leads first to numbness and then to frostbite if unchecked. It even happens in air conditioning - I could be hanging out at home and catch a chill, and my toes will go white.

I'd gotten in the habit of staying inside in the winter, but I was tired of missing out on snowy photographic opportunities. I decided to sign up for a winter Yellowstone workshop, and I started investing in better winter gear. Before the big trip to Yellowstone, I thought I'd do a test run in the Badlands since it was so much closer to home, and I'd never shot the unique scenery in winter.

I thought the snow would be great for contrast in the Badlands, and I aimed for capturing sunset light with a colorful sky. I had to arrive to the park early to scope out my location, but I got there a little too early! I found my spot in plenty of time, set up… and waited. In 12 degree Fahrenheit temperature.

My Raynaud's can start to kick in when the temp drops below 40, so 12 degrees was a drastic difference. I knew it was going to be cold, of course, so I had two warming packets in my shoes. I soon discovered, however, that they need AIR to stay activated. They started nice and warm, but after suffocating in my Gortex snowboots for a while, they stopped working.

Slowly my feet began to chill, the freezing temps creeping in and spreading. I started stomping my feet around and doing all kinds of movement to keep me warm, but it just had no effect on my feet. Stubbornness kicked in though – I was going to see this through!

As the sky began to change color, I lost all awareness of my cold feet. All I could focus on was the stunning scenery before me. THIS is what I was out here for! It is still one of my favorite moments in the Badlands. I had the park to myself (no shocker there, hello winter!), and the sky was the prettiest I had ever seen it.

I shot and shot and shot until all the color was gone… then packed up quickly and headed back to my car to get warm! I drove off and by the time I reached the next viewpoint not five minutes away, my feet were in so much pain I had to pull over, rip off my shoes and rub my feet to try and make the pain go away. My toes were whiter than I'd ever seen them.

While shooting, my feet had apparently gone so numb that I didn't realize how bad they were, and the high from the gorgeous sunset was an additional distraction. But once that blood tried to flow back into my feet? OUCH! Thankfully it was only the early stages of frostbite, and my feet recovered on their own. I learned my lesson the hard way that day, and I now take much better care of my extremities in cold weather. Trust me, I have no plans to ever experience full-blown frostbite!

Sadly my Raynaud's symptoms are getting worse every year, but for now, I'm thankful to get out and enjoy snowy weather any time it's safe for me to do so. I'll still shoot as many winter images as possible while I still can.

The Flow of Time A distractingly beautiful winter sunset at Door Trail – Badlands National Park, USA

December 2015

CRAP, WHICH ROAD WAS IT?

Bear Butte | South Dakota, United States

EXPOSURE
Shutter 1/25 sec. | Aperture f/22 | ISO 200

CAMERA GEAR
Nikon D810 | Nikkor 28-70 f/2.8 | Shot @ 70mm

december 2015

I grew up in the Black Hills and have lived here my whole life, except for a few years when I lived in California to get my photography degree. So you would think I'd know all the secret local spots, right?

Yeah, not so much. I'm slightly embarrassed that I've had to ask around for directions to the hidden spots that should be known to "locals" like me. I've even had to go so far as to get directions from an out-of-stater! **(See the "Temperamental Ice" story on page 66.)**

This ended up being the case on a venture in December of 2015. Perusing Facebook, I saw fellow photographers from the area posting pictures of a haunting rustic barn. In the background was the distinct landmark of Bear Butte.

What?!? Bear Butte? That's LOCAL!

I'd photographed Bear Butte before – why didn't I know where this barn was? I thought I'd already shot all the best angles of Bear Butte… I NEEDED to find this barn.

I reached out to one of my friends who'd posted a picture and asked if they'd be so kind as to take me to this mystery barn. He was happy to, and we decided to make it an afternoon winter photography adventure that would end with sunset at the barn location.

It was a typical December day when we headed out, with snow on the ground and plenty of sunshine. We first looked for the bison herd that roams near Bear Butte, hoping to get some wildlife shots. Unfortunately we couldn't get a view of the bison with Bear Butte composed well in the background, but it was no less enjoyable watching the furry beasts dig for the grass.

The clock was ticking, so we headed for the barn. It was a good thing we took off when we did, because my friend was having a hard time remembering which road to take! We drove for quite a bit along one road before he sheepishly admitted that he must have taken the wrong one. So we backtracked to the main road, and he confidently drove down another road.

> "The golden hour light hit and it was magical."

Then it happened again! At this point I was beginning to think we were lost, but we did eventually find our way to the correct road. In his defense, I would have never thought the road we ended up on would be the route to this barn – it felt like it would be too far away. But we thankfully arrived in time to catch the sun setting directly behind the butte.

Finally, I would get to shoot the mystery barn! The rustic building was so picturesque with the snow on the ground and the butte providing the perfect backdrop; then the golden hour light hit and it was magical. There couldn't have been a more perfect moment or a more perfect image to close out the end of 2015.

Life in South Dakota An elusive country barn known only to "locals" somewhere by Bear Butte – Near Sturgis, South Dakota, USA   December 2015

WHAT THE FOX IS GOING ON?

Yellowstone National Park | Wyoming, United States

EXPOSURE **CAMERA GEAR**
Shutter 1/1000 sec. | Aperture f/7.1 | ISO 800   Nikon D610 | Nikkor 300 f/2.8 | 420mm w/ Nikkor TC -14E II

february 2016

I had been to Yellowstone National Park numerous times, but never in winter. That finally changed in 2015 when I took advantage of an opportunity and signed on for an adventure with what was then the Yellowstone Park Foundation. I was finally getting to visit the park while it was blanketed in snow!

Never had I felt such peaceful solitude when I was in the park. To be able to watch Old Faithful erupt with just the members of my group instead of throngs of tourists, not to mention the effect of freezing temperatures… it was mind blowing. I will never forget seeing the super-heated steam billow and rise to meet the cresting sun on that calm and almost tranquil morning. It was so quiet and still, all we could hear was the roar of the geyser.

It was freezing outside, but for that one moment your mind forgets the numbness in your hands and coldness in your feet, and you just feel pure joy.

Instantly, I was in love with Yellowstone in winter. I was so in love that I "conned" eight of my friends to go back with me the next year for a workshop led by me. I say "conned" because I really just wanted enough people to share the cost of getting our own snow coach with a hired driver, and to be able to take as much time as we wanted to explore the park and take pics. Hey, it was a fair deal!

The highlight of 2016 for me was the foxes! They seem to rule the park in the winter. By the end of the trip we'd seen almost 20 different foxes - unprecedented for me.

One fox in particular stands out when thinking back. We were headed out of the park when we spotted a fox about 500 feet off in the distance. We lucked out and he was on the hunt! Watching him pounce headfirst into the snow was such an incredible moment – this is something you think you'll only ever see on National Geographic with David Attenborough narrating. The entire group was in awe as we watched his graceful hunt in the snow.

The coach stopped, and as we got out the fox stopped what he was doing, looked up… and walked straight for us. We couldn't believe it!

Within a minute he was right next to the road. With his uncommon behavior, we weren't sure what to expect next. He stopped… and peed on a tree. Ha! And then this beautiful fox trotted confidently across the road.

My acclaimed "Year of the Fox" image is from that encounter, just as he was headed down the other side of the snowy road.

When we got back in the coach, our driver was stunned. He had NEVER seen a fox behave that way.

We'll take that luck any day!

Nature's bathroom! ▶
A Yellowstone snow coach ▼

Year of the Fox Attention, fox crossing! – Yellowstone National Park, USA

February 2016

THEY HAVE WHAT NOW?!?!

Badlands National Park | South Dakota, United States

EXPOSURE
Shutter 1/500 sec. | Aperture f/6.3 | ISO 640

CAMERA GEAR
Nikon D810 | Nikkor 300 f/2.8 | 600mm w/ Nikkor TC-20E III

may 2016

The average person would assume that a local to the Black Hills and Badlands area, such as myself, would know things about the wildlife in the area. Bison are not just big fluffy cows and you shouldn't get too close to them? Check. That adorable rattle sound isn't someone's happy baby, but a rattlesnake warning you away? Double check. Prairie dogs in the Badlands have disease ridden fleas and can give you the plague? Che… wait, WHAT?!?!

We'll come back to that.

I really did think I was quite knowledgeable about all the wildlife roaming the Black Hills and Badlands area – they were, after all, the stomping grounds of my childhood and early photography career. So I was completely surprised in 2016 to see my friends posting pictures of pint-sized owls, and to discover they'd taken those pictures in one of my absolute favorite nearby places, Badlands National Park!

What were these adorable little creatures, and where could I find them??? One friend filled me in, saying they were burrowing owls and they lived in prairie dog towns.

I'd photographed prairie dogs before… how had I never seen these winged little things flitting around? Well it turns out that the burrowing owls use the prairie dog mounds for their nests, so they're almost always on the ground. And since their coloring is similar to the prairie dogs, they blend right in. Chances were that I'd looked right at one and just not realized I was looking at a different animal.

> "Prairie dogs… can give you the PLAGUE?"

I was skeptical of this; I have terrific vision, eyes as good as an eagle! But discovering the animal existed gave me the magical powers I needed to see the little creatures. On my next trip to the Badlands, sure enough, I spotted a burrowing owl perched on a prairie dog mound. I realized they probably had been around all along, but I'd been so focused on the prairie dogs that I didn't realize another critter was about.

As you can see by the picture, the owls are quite small. At least my eagle vision was validated, since I'd spotted the little owl all the way from my car! Even knowing what I was looking at, my brain still wanted to automatically think it was a prairie dog, as they blend in so well. But I'd found the cute fluff ball, and was finally going to photograph one!

Quickly I grabbed my gear and got my settings, then slowly made my way out into the "Prairie Dog Town," navigating slowly and carefully around the mounds to approach the little owl. I stopped at a spot that the feathered critter seemed comfortable with, then sat down on the ground so I could shoot at his level. I got this adorable one-legged shot and was excited to rush home and share it with my friends!

Shortly after I proudly posted my picture, my friend Deb informed me that prairie dogs get fleas, and fleas carry the bacteria that causes plague. Not only had I strolled through a possibly flea infested field, I'd plopped right down in it.

I was very, very lucky to not have brought home some new mini pets that day. I think my saving grace was that it was early spring and maybe the little buggers weren't hatched yet. Next time I visit the prairie dogs and burrowing owls, I'll do it with an even bigger zoom lens!

Owl Be Seeing You The adorable little critter that almost got me diseased – Badlands National Park, USA

May 2016

Date with a Bunny Memoirs of my lovely date with Mr. Cottontail Rabbit – Wind Cave National Park, USA

May 2016

THE BUNNY WHO SAVED ME

Wind Cave National Park | South Dakota, United States

EXPOSURE
Shutter 1/320 sec. | Aperture f/8 | ISO 640

CAMERA GEAR
Nikon D810 | Nikkor 70-200 f/4.0 | Shot @ 185mm

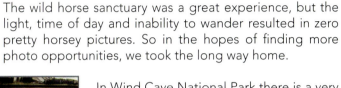

This image doesn't quite fit my normal wildlife subject matter. I shoot grizzlies and bison, not bunnies! Regardless, I will never forget this little guy who saved me from a miserable fate, and neither will my friend Dan, who was NOT saved by the bunny.

Shall we start at the beginning?

I'd booked a tour for my mom and I at the wild horse sanctuary in Hot Springs, not far from home. She had to cancel, so I invited my photographer friend Dan. We decided to make a day of it, planning to get up early enough so that we'd have time to explore and stop for photos on the way to Hot Springs. Dan first took me to the little town of Ardmore; I had never been there before but had seen pictures and was excited to go explore all the run down, dilapidated buildings.

In all my excitement to check out a new location, I forgot May was tick season and wasn't exactly cautious while tromping around the tall grasses and brambling bushes in the area.

Finally satisfied with our exploration of Ardmore, we hopped in the car to head off to the horse sanctuary. On the long drive, something fuzzy kept dangling in my face and it was driving me nuts! Irritated, I finally pulled off my stocking cap to find I had a TICK ON ME!

I might have freaked out. Just a little. I definitely had the heebie jeebies the rest of the day!

▲ Dilapidated Ardmore

The wild horse sanctuary was a great experience, but the light, time of day and inability to wander resulted in zero pretty horsey pictures. So in the hopes of finding more photo opportunities, we took the long way home.

In Wind Cave National Park there is a very old, stunning bridge, and since we were in no rush, Dan wanted to stop, hike to the base and take some pictures.

We started walking down the overgrown path, and well, all I could think was "ticks, ticks, ticks, EWW!" I wussed out and told Dan I'd wait at the car. Back by the car, I saw this bunny! Figuring I had a little time to kill while Dan was off shooting, I got down on the ground and had a wonderful play date with Mr. Bunny. He was so beautiful and I was surprised he didn't hop away; I got such a close look at him! I love how you can see the delicate veins in his ear.

Dan ended up shooting that bridge for a whole HOUR. Yes, I spent an hour crawling around taking photos of a bunny rabbit. If not for that rabbit, I likely would have gotten bored and braved the trek down to the bridge.

So how did Mr. Bunny save me? Well, the next day Dan called to tell me I had made a good choice to stay at the car. Not only did he not get any great pics… he also returned with an outbreak of poison ivy.

Thanks Mr. Bunny.

TAKE THE RISK, OR NOT?

Grand Teton National Park | Wyoming, United States

EXPOSURE
Shutter 1/4 sec. | Aperture f/11 | ISO 400

CAMERA GEAR
Nikon D810 | Nikkor 28-70 f/2.8 | Shot @ 32mm

2016 may

I was excited to check out Schwabacher Landing since it had beeen closed when my mom and I visited in 2014. I'd read that a beaver is often spotted there and hoped to capture an image of the critter. I had scoped out the area the day before and had already picked out the prime spot where I hoped to plant my tripod. I knew since it was before Memorial Day, it wouldn't be too crazy with a lot of people early in the morning. But just in case, I planned to arrive well before o'dark thirty.

When I pulled in the next morning, I was surprised to see I wasn't the first one there. One other car had beaten me, but I was actually glad that I wouldn't be completely alone out there in the dark. As you may have read **(see "Geysers Aren't Afraid of the Dark," page 63)**, I'm a little bit unnerved by the dark. OK, OK… I'm not just unnerved, I'm downright afraid of the dark.

I headed down to the end of the trail, past the beaver dam, and found my spot with the help of my headlamp. The narrow bit of light wasn't much help for composing my shot in the dark, but I managed and settled in to wait for a hopefully epic sunrise.

As it got lighter out, more people shuffled in and the grumbles began. You see, it's a big pond, but there are only a few narrow spots with a clear view of Grand Teton's peak – the highest – looming through the trees. People were giving me expectant looks to invite them into my bubble, but I go with the stance that hey, I got up early, I'm there first and this is my job, so you can wait until I'm done.

After a while the grumbles did get to me. Now that we had some light, I looked around and saw a possible spot for a shot over by the beaver dam. I liked the shape of the dam, and it looked like I'd have a nice view of the mountain. There were also some cool looking dead white trees in the water that I could put in the foreground. But did I really want to give up my prime real estate?

I took a gamble, grabbed my gear and left my spot. The second I left, people crowded into my abandoned space. I was SOL if the new spot didn't work out. Thankfully, it did – as I settled in and set up, I saw I had hit a gold mine. The beaver was actually out to work on the dam! I hadn't been able to see him from the other spot.

The light was still low, forcing me to use a shutter speed that's not optimal for wildlife. I carefully composed my shot with the beaver in the lower-third crosshair, and he magically stayed still! The gorgeous morning alpen glow was still painting the peaks and I got this shot.

I kept shooting a bit after the pink started to fade, while the other photographers started to head out. Some of them passed me and gave me curious looks, wondering why I was still shooting. I casually mentioned I was shooting the beaver with the sunrise. That peaked some interest, but by the time anyone looked, the beaver had gone.

I was so glad I'd taken the gamble on that spot and captured something unique, and was blessed with a moment – and a photograph – that is unforgettable.

Busy Beaver The famed beaver getting an early start at Schwabacher Landing – Grand Teton National Park, USA

May 2016

Flow Back In Time A truly unique and amazing image of Mormon Row, in my humble opinion ;) – Grand Teton National Park, USA

IN FOR A TREAT

Grand Teton National Park | Wyoming, United States

EXPOSURE
Shutter 1.3 sec. | Aperture f/16 | ISO 250

CAMERA GEAR
Nikon D810 | Nikkor 17-35 f/2.8 | Shot @ 20mm

may 2016

I had been dreaming of going back to the Tetons ever since my epic year of shooting there in 2014. **(See stories on pages 42, 56, 58, 60… I think that's it…)** When I'm missing a place, I tend to hop online and check hotel prices, usually ending up sad when the prices just aren't in the budget. So when I found reasonable prices for the Tetons in the spring of 2016, I couldn't NOT go!

One spot I'd never tried for sunset was Mormon Row, an area with rustic old farm buildings where I'd photographed some adorable coyote pups in 2014 **(ooh, that's the Tetons story I forgot, on page 44!)**. I pulled into the park after an eight-hour drive from Rapid City, first checking out nearby Schwabacher Landing to scope out a spot for shooting sunrise the next morning. That didn't take long, so I arrived at Mormom with plenty of time to explore the barns.

I was happy to see I was the only person there! I love it when I have a location to myself, and I took my time scouring the scene to find my favorite composition. They'd apparently had a wet spring season, and I noticed an irrigation ditch full of water that I hadn't seen two years before. I walked the ditch, admiring the sky's reflection in the water, and found the perfect spot! The waterway made a lovely S curve that drew my eye to one of the barns, with the dramatic Tetons as a stunning backdrop. Time to shoot!

Ever wonder what happens behind the scenes of an image like this? I still laugh thinking about my set-up for this shot! I had to perch on a small concrete wall and extend one tripod leg INTO the water, which had me a little worried after my camera had gone for a swim two years earlier **(see "No Time for Insurance," page 52)**. But I'd learned my lesson and had insurance this time, so I relaxed and settled in to enjoy the view.

As I waited for the light to change, other photographers started to arrive. I stood and watched them do the same dance I'd done earlier, scouring the area for the best composition. I had to hide a gleeful grin as they jealously paced the road behind me, glaring with desire to be in my spot. Ha! I won't lie, it felt good that my preparedness had paid off. It pays to get to your spot early!

At that point, however, I thought I might only get a nice black and white composition, as the clouds didn't look like they'd let any sunset light through for color. It's always disappointing to not get any color, but the scene was still pretty. Everyone settled in to get whatever shot they could.

> "Ever wonder what happens behind the scenes?"

It was then that a car raced up, and a young guy jumped out. He happily ran over to set up his camera in an unoccupied spot, and made a bit of an announcement to everyone. "We are in for a treat!" he said. "I just came from the other side and there are NO clouds [blocking the sunset]! It should start turning red any minute!"

And thankfully, he was right! It still didn't go bright red as all our hearts seemed to desire, but in the end I absolutely love the scene that the light and my composition created. I had set out to create a unique image of this location, something unlike any of the millions of photographs that had been done before, and I succeeded. To this day, I still have not seen an image like mine, and it makes me proud.

DAY OF DISCOVERY

Custer State Park | South Dakota, United States

EXPOSURE
Shutter 1/10 sec. | Aperture f/16 | ISO 400

CAMERA GEAR
Nikon D810 | Nikkor 70-200 f/4.0 | Shot @ 82mm

2016 july

Several years ago, my adventure buddy Toni and I realized that even though we'd grown up in the Black Hills, we really hadn't explored the area like we do when we travel. We decided we'd better do something about that!

I'd been wanting to do a sunset picture from the top of Little Devils Tower, a cliff I've always seen from the Black Elk Peak (formerly Harney Peak) trail. According to other locals we'd grown up with, the trail to Little Devils Tower was also where you started out to find one of the best kept secrets of the Black Hills at that time: Poet's Table.

By what we'd heard, some long ago employee at Sylvan Lake had carried a table, chairs and cabinet up to a hidden overlook in Custer State Park in the late 60s. Since then, any who found it had left their own writings and memoirs behind. We had directions from older siblings, but after researching a bit we realized those wouldn't work – the original trail for Little Devils Tower had moved! So directions such as "turn by the third downed tree" were certainly not going to help us.

We did manage to find a more recent account of how to head in the right direction, so we took off on our hike early enough in the day to let us explore and hopefully find the secret spot. Thankfully we did, because less than two years later, some idiots thought they needed to "protect" nature by hauling the table, chairs and cabinet out of the hills. Their efforts instead destroyed this treasured spot that had survived for over 40 years.

People suck sometimes. But they can also be amazing – members of the community came together to carry up a newly built, smaller table and chair so younger generations can still enjoy it.

Back to the hike! After Poet's Table, we headed back to the Little Devils Tower trail. I'd only done the hike once at sunrise, but it was Toni's first time ever hiking the trail. We both fell in love with the unique views it offered and how stunning it was in warm light.

Just before reaching the top, you walk up to an incredible view of the Cathedral Spires right in front of you! The spires are part of an area known as The Needles, distinctive granite formations unique to Custer State Park. The hike just gets better, as to reach the top you have to climb up through worn crevices in the rocky peak, doing a bit of "bouldering." It's a bit scary at first, but totally fun and worth the view.

▲ Switched! Looking at Black Elk Peak from Little Devils Tower instead of vice-versa

▲ The Poet's Table of days past, before it was destroyed by vandals :(

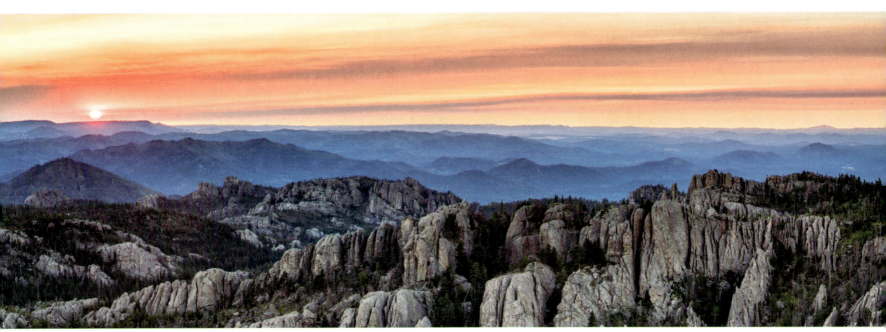

Heart of the Hills A smoky sunset over the granite peaks of the Black Hills (multi-image panoramic) – Custer State Park of South Dakota, USA   July 2016

And what a view it is! With The Needles and Black Elk Peak in one direction, and a clear view of The Black Hills out to the plains in the other direction, it's a breathtaking panorama.

We clambered around for a while and took some celebratory pictures, but once that initial excitement faded, I realized I was out of luck. There were no clouds in the sky, and clouds are usually a requirement for epic sunset photos. No clouds = no color. We decided to hang out until sunset, but I wasn't too hopeful. Still, I'd hauled my camera all this way! I set up for a photo, planning to use my handy panoramic tripod head.

We spent our time waiting with our backs to the sun, watching the golden light hit the Cathedral Spires, and continued to watch as the shadow of our mountain crept up the spires. We'd waited to turn around and take in the sunset view all at once, knowing that even though it may not be epic, it would still be beautiful.

So when we turned around to wispy clouds and a soft orange sky over blue mountains, I was shocked. It was stunning!

While shooting the sunset, I realized the wind was blowing in the direction of the clouds... and they weren't actually clouds at all. It was smoke from a forest fire. It was a sad realization, but I'll never forget the unique scene the smoke created – one that cannot be replicated. I'm certainly not hoping for another fire! We later found out the smoke had come from the Bighorn Mountains in Wyoming.

The smoke seemed to be the portent of doom, as the end of our excursion was a bit stressful! We realized, as it was getting dark, that we only had one head lamp between us. (I blame Toni. I swear I told her to grab the flashlight!) Once that worry set in, I started to also worry that I hadn't locked the car, and since my door had a code pad, I'd purposely left the keys IN the car. Needless to say, we made it back to the car in record time!

The car was locked, of course. I really have to stop worrying so much.

Another side note to this image – I was in my art booth at a show in 2019 and a guy came in and said he was told to look for the mountain goat in this image. I was so confused! Somebody else found a mountain goat in my image that I didn't know about? Intrigued, the gentleman and I searched the print I had on display... and finally found it! I think we only found it because the fine-art print was sized to 20"x 60." Talk about quality! The goat was still only 1/4 inch big, so my image had to be tack sharp to find it in the texture of the rock. I was pretty amazed at what someone found in my image. How cool.

▲ **Taking in a late afternoon view of Cathedral Spires**
(Pardon the goofy hats, we're both a bit sensitive to the sun!)

WE'RE GOING ON AN ADVENTURE!

Franz Josef Glacier | Westland Tai Poutini National Park | South Island, New Zealand

EXPOSURE
Shutter 1/320 sec. | Aperture f/16 | ISO 400

CAMERA GEAR
Nikon D810 | Nikkor 14-24 f/2.8 | Shot @ 14mm

march 2017

I'm obsessed with glaciers. It all started when I had my first incredible experience with a glacier during my high school exchange trip to New Zealand. Back then we hiked to the foot of the Fox Glacier and got up-close-and-personal with it, walking onto the ice and exploring the alien landscape. I'd never imaged glaciers could have their own valleys and tunnels and waterfalls! It was impressive, to say the least.

So when my husband and I planned our big dream trip to New Zealand a few years ago, I hoped to recreate my awesome glacial hiking experience for the two of us.

As big Lord of the Rings fans, my husband and I had been dreaming for years of going to the amazing filming locations in New Zealand. We finally saved up enough money to plan our dream trip for March of 2017, and it was going to be EPIC! We had so many things planned! Just like Bilbo, we were going on an adventure!

Best laid plans, right? Our "epic" adventures were ruined as our planned excursions got rained out again and again and again. We made the best of the days, but I'm not gonna lie, it was disappointing. So when it finally came time to visit a glacier – Franz Joseph, not Fox – we decided to bite the bullet and splurge on a helicopter ride. This would take us to land right by the glacier, instead of us hiking to one like I'd done 20 years before.

It turned out that you could no longer hike inland to this particular glacier anyway! What the f! In just two decades the glacier had receded so far that you couldn't hike to it, only to a cliffside lookout point. This is one of the saddest things to see with glaciers, but

▲ These happily-ever-after Tolkien fans finally made it to Middle Earth!
(Wow, I fit well in a Hobbit home...)

we took it as a sign that we were meant to enjoy a fancy and impressive (and super expensive) helicopter ride to the glacier.

Now if only the weather would hold out…

We arrived to the area and booked an early morning chopper flight to Franz Joseph Glacier the next day. After checking in we headed to nearby Fox Glacier for sunset, and the lovely not-rainy weather bode well for our helicopter ride in the morning. Everything was finally falling into place!

I awoke that morning bright-eyed and bushy-tailed with excitement in my step! I bounded to the window of our room… only to find it overcast, foggy, and just downright gloomy. It appeared that once again the weather would beat us. Curse you, Mother Nature!

And sure enough, our helicopter flight got cancelled and we had to reschedule for the next day. That would be our absolute last chance, as we were checking out and moving on to our next location afterward.

Seeing our disappointment, the staff tried to perk us up by suggesting we head out to hike Robert's Point Track, a local trail that overlooks the glacier. We didn't have anything else planned, so we thought, "Why not?"

Since we were bummed, we didn't think much of just taking off to go on the hike and didn't stop to grab snacks or water. Normally we research a hike to see how long it is and what we need to do to prepare, but we'd already done a couple of all-day 12-mile hikes on this trip. Pfft, we weren't worried about this one.

Apparently, we should have been! I mean, the signs on the trail warning of DEATH should have been at least a red flag for the fitness level this trail required. But like I said, we'd already conquered

Glacial Perspective A distant tour group hiking across the Franz Josef Glacier – Westland Tai Poutini National Park, New Zealand

March 2017

some big hikes on this trip. How bad could it be? C'mon, we've hiked MOUNTAINS! We can do this! We pushed forward.

If I had been on my own, I tell you, I would have turned around! I was still tired from aforementioned hikes, and lugging along my camera bag didn't help. My hubby took pity on me and switched out our bags, motivating me to keep going. "Wow, this thing's heavy!" he said. I simply replied, "Yeah, I know." Professional camera gear is not light!

We eventually made it to the top and had a magical moment when we saw another hiker offering to share their apples! I was too tired to even speak, just needed to catch my breath for a minute, so my thoughtful hubby grabbed me one. Thanks honey!

The final view was lackluster, but hey, the apple was amazing!

The next morning, we woke to clear blue skies. Finally, the flight was a go and we'd get to do something epic!

It's amazing how a little distance alters your perspective. From far away in the air, the Franz Joseph Glacier didn't look that big. When you see the markers that show how much of it has melted over the years, your brain wants to write it off as not being that much, no big deal.

But when you realize the little black specks moving across the glacier are PEOPLE, your perspective shifts. That was about to be US! This was going to be awesome. I was still appreciating the

Persistence Colorful moss and algae growing on rock formations in the valley below the Franz Josef Glacier – Westland Tai Poutini National Park, New Zealand — March 2017

EXPOSURE Shutter 1/30 sec. | Aperture f/14 | ISO 400   **CAMERA GEAR** Nikon D810 | Nikkor 14-24 f/2.8 | Shot @ 14mm

new perspective as the helicopter approached the glacier and landed right ON the ice. How crazy!

This tour company had their job down to a science. Glaciers are constantly shifting as they melt, re-freeze and melt again, usually melting more than freezing, sadly. The tour guides had already gone out and carved out a safe trek across the glacier. They have their work cut out for them, keeping people secure on this glacier. Normal glaciers are full of dangerous crags and cracks, and we were told this was also the steepest glacier offering commercial tours.

Reassured by their precautions, we geared up and headed out on the hike. I was so happy to be back, getting an awesome new experience at Franz Josef Glacier with the bonus of enjoying it with my husband, plus capturing the adventure at my more experienced, professional level of photography.

I lagged behind the group a bit, stopping for photos when I could. I was stunned at one point when we came upon a view of the group ahead of us crossing the glacier. I don't normally like to have people in my photos, but there's no way to convey the scale of this glacier without them. I appropriately titled the image "Glacial Perspective."

I was sad when the tour was over, but glad that one of our experiences was finally full of sunshine.

Off to the next adventure!

The treacherous Robert's Point Track... not a beginner's hike! ▶

"Three people have died on Robert's Point Track..." Say whaaaaaat?!?

▲ Chopper delivery directly to the glacier! ▶

▶ Looking cool on Franz Joseph Glacier

A Beautiful Mess Low tide sunrise at a popular fjord area, Milford Sound – New Zealand

March 2017

GLAD WE BOUGHT INSURANCE...

Milford Sound | South Island, New Zealand

EXPOSURE
Shutter 1/8 sec. | Aperture f/16 | ISO 200

CAMERA GEAR
Nikon D810 | Nikkor 28-70 f/2.8 | Shot @ 40mm

march 2017

My first time to New Zealand was in high school on a foreign exchange trip. It was an unforgettable experience for a teen, but there was one distinct disappointment – the road was closed to Milford Sound and we didn't get to see one of the most well-known locations in New Zealand.

Fast forward 20 years to 2017 and I was finally going to see it on a dream vacation with my husband! We couldn't afford to stay right in Milford, so we had a two-hour drive to get there. My poor hubby Adam, bless his heart, got up with me in the middle of the night so we could drive there to catch a sunrise photo. We got up and loaded into our rental car in 3 am darkness. I drove, and Adam soon fell fast asleep. Good thing I was used to navigating on my own, thanks to my trusty GPS!

Can we take a second to appreciate GPS? Where would I be without it? Heck, how did we ever live without it?

Moving on. We arrived at Milford Sound just as it was getting light out. I parked the car, kissed my hubby good night and off I went to find the perfect spot! I enjoyed the exploration in the quiet morning, having the area almost all to myself. I'd started with composing some shots near the car, but it was low tide and the foreground was too busy. I ended up trekking a little further out, closer to the water and out of view from the parking lot.

As I worked my scene, I heard a horn start honking. I stopped and listened. I thought maybe Adam had accidentally locked himself out of the car, but I didn't hear him call my name, so I assumed someone else was doing the honking.

A little while later, I noticed Adam was standing next to me. "Someone hit our car," he said tiredly. I laughed in disbelief, thinking he was joking, pulling my leg. He wasn't.

While he was sleeping in the car, a small RV had felt the need to park riiiiiiiight next to us, even though the back of the parking lot – where campers are supposed to park – was pretty empty. They apparently didn't know how to maneuver the big vehicle too well, and they sideswiped our rental! Sheesh. Thankfully we had insurance, but even though it wasn't our fault, we still had to pay around $180.

Unfortunately, the crash not only ruined the calming, serene mood of the morning, but it ruined the day and ended up being a harbinger of bad luck for the next day! Stressed and annoyed by the wreck, we skipped the Milford Sound cruise we'd thought about taking that day. We just wanted to leave after that mess, and we were scheduled for a boat cruise of Doubtful Sound the next day anyway.

Well, that cruise bombed as well. It rained the entire day and we could hardly see anything on the tour. The captain kept saying how lucky we were to get all this moisture and see waterfalls, but I was not amused.

We had great moments that saved the trip, thankfully, like when we visited Hobbiton. Yes, we are big LOR fans, and fellow fans seem to know how to park! Hooray for nerds!

Winner of "The Most Idiotic Parking Job EVER!"

BEAR-LY HOLDING ON

Grand Teton National Park | Wyoming, United States

EXPOSURE
Shutter 1/2000 sec. | Aperture f/6.3 | ISO 400

CAMERA GEAR
Nikon D610 | Nikkor 300 f/2.8

2017 may

A photographer friend and I had decided to meet up in the Tetons in early spring to hopefully find some bears. It's a good time to spot them as they're emerging from hibernation, hungry and ready to forage, and the snow still in the high elevations makes them easier to spot.

We spent days searching and searching, but had no luck. We started to despair that we'd never spot one of the majestic grizzlies. Our dreams of beautiful bear photos were fading before our eyes!

As luck would have it, I then heard back from a friend I'd reached out to who lives in the area. I'd been looking for his local perspective on where the bears hang out, and he was late getting back to me because he'd been out of town. But just as we were ready to give up on the area, he pointed us in the right direction. We made a plan to check out the new spot the next day.

We started that day with new vigor! Refreshed with caffeine in our systems, we headed out to the new location. I felt a slight urge to use the ladies room as we were heading out, but I thought (stupidly) nah, I'll be fine until we reach a restroom. We drove for about 20 minutes with no luck – no bears, no businesses, nothing. As you can imagine, bumpy, curvy, snowy roads don't help the urge to pee! Then we turned a corner and finally came to a lodge. "Yes!" I thought, "I can use their bathroom!"

They were closed. Aaaaaarrrrrggghhhhh!

I couldn't bear it any longer. (See what I did there? Bear it? OK, moving on…) I fessed up to my friend that I really, really had to go. Since we once again hadn't seen a bear, we gave in to defeat and turned around to head back to our hotel, and whatever toilet we could find!

As we rounded the corner leaving the lodge, what do we see but a grizzly bear! He was munching away at the fresh green grass peeking through the snow on the side of the road. The excitement level in the car skyrocketed, and thankfully my urge to pee did not. I forgot all about my need for a restroom and we spent the next hour following the bear as he slowly wandered along the road. We'd had fresh snow the day before and it just added to the pristine beauty of the moment.

Eventually my bladder won out and I told my friend we'd finally have to leave the bear to his foraging. We headed back and I finally got to take care of business!

To add insult to injury, the next day my bladder acted up again, right in the middle of another bear search. We even saw another bear that day! It was weird, I never have trouble with needing to find a bathroom so much. I guess my full bladder is a lucky charm for finding bears? Ha!

I Need My Coffee A sleepy Grizzly Bear meandering in the snow, digging for green grass – Grand Teton National Park, USA

A TOTALITY EPIC ADVENTURE

Total Solar Eclipse | Somewhere near the Wyoming border, United States

EXPOSURE
Shutter 1/100 & 1/1000 sec. | Aperture f/5.6 | ISO 800

CAMERA GEAR
Nikon D810 | Nikkor 300 f/2.8 | 420mm w/ Nikkor TC -14E II

2017 July

I'd heard of this eclipse thing a year or so before it happened, and honestly, I was pretty "meh" about the whole thing. I figured hey, my home town was in the 99% viewing zone, so that had to be good enough, right?

Wrong.

About a month before the eclipse, I was enjoying my morning tea when I came across a TedTalk about the eclipse. I thought, what the heck, why not watch it? I watched it... and soon learned how badly I had screwed myself.

A total solar eclipse is completely different from other eclipses, and you can NOT see the actual eclipse unless you are in the 100% totality zone. I was scheduled to work that day... and the totality zone was 150 miles away.

Thankfully my amazing boss happened to be a fan of all things space-related, so she let me take the day off. Yes! Next up, I needed to figure out HOW to photograph an eclipse. And that's when I found out I might truly be SOL.

Just as staring at the eclipse without proper glasses can burn out your retinas, taking a successful picture of the sun itself can burn out your camera sensors without an insanely strong filter. Of course, the photographers who'd realized how cool an event this would be right away had already bought up ALL of the filters. There wasn't even solar film available if I wanted to go old school. Nothing. Nada.

As a last minute shot in the dark, I asked my Facebook world if they had anything I could use. First someone suggested I get a piece of welding glass (the piece worn in the helmet to protect the welder's eyes), and I was assured this would work great for photography. I found a piece at a local hardware store, then built my own holder to keep the glass in place in front of my lens. I excitedly tested the set-up with a picture of the sun. And... it failed.

The glass just wasn't quality enough to be able to take a sharp photo through it, and my lens picked up every little scratch and ding in the glass – things that wouldn't get in the way for a welder or casual viewer, but just didn't work for photography. Shoot. (Or not shoot, in this case...)

I turned to Facebook and was excited to see that my photographer friend Dan had solar film he didn't need, and he said that I could have it!!! ...if I could drive to Nebraska to get it, that is. I was ready to jump in my car the day before the eclipse and drive all day to get it, when, as luck would have it, my hubby and his mom happened to be on the way back from a

Eerie eclipse shadows taking over the sky in Wyoming
▼

Best Day Off Ever! Multi-image composite (inner suns 1/100, outer suns 1/1,000 with solar film) of the stages of a solar eclipse – Wyoming, USA   July 2017

trip and were passing through Nebraska! They kindly went 20 minutes out of their way to save me the trip.

The stars were aligning and I was finally free and ready to go shoot the eclipse!

I didn't want to go alone, so I called my best friend Toni and conned her into taking that Monday off to go see the eclipse with me. She'd had the same initial reaction to the eclipse as me – meh, no big deal, 99% should be plenty good for viewing, right? I launched into my Ted-Talk-educated spiel and infected her with my excitement. She quickly requested a vacation day to join my adventure. :-)

We wanted to be sure to have plenty of time to set up for the 10:20 am eclipse. We had a three hour drive ahead of us to reach our viewing destination of somewhere-out-near-the-border-of-Wyoming, so we hit the highway by 6:30 am. We'd never seen so many cars heading to Wyoming at the same time! We got a little worried when we reached Lusk and actually hit a traffic jam outside the little town! (If you've ever been to Lusk, you know how bizarre this was.) We thankfully made it through and reached the road we planned to take to find a viewing spot. This was a highway that cuts through hills and farming country in Wyoming, and we usually pass less than five cars on the whole 50 mile stretch.

Not today! There was steady traffic and cars parked randomly all along the road, plus private groups camped out in the fields. It was unreal! After a while we found a pull-off on a curve that looked like it had potential for some foreground; I always think of the foreground when composing my shot, but I soon realized the foreground wouldn't matter with this eclipse – the sun was too high in the sky. **A future note for photographers:** find the high ground with a landscape view, and you might get some cool shots before the eclipse as the light changes. More on that later.

We parked and thankfully had plenty of time to set up. With the popularity of this event, a couple more cars joined our area and we had the company of like-minded enthusiasts. We all hung out in camping chairs and ate the snacks we packed, waiting for things to get interesting.

▲ CRAZY traffic backed up In Lusk, WY

I started to get the urge to pee. Of course. We'd rushed through the morning, so worried about getting to our spot early… and even though I'd not drank my usual pot of tea on purpose, I still had to go. Dang it. Well, I'd buck up and get it done right away so this annoyance wouldn't ruin my experience!

I wasn't sure where to go. We saw a couple of guys disappear into a valley on the other side of the road… well, that spot's taken! Our side of the road was much more open, but there were a few big brambly bushes down from the road a bit. I walked down to test how much they blocked, and when my friend said she couldn't see me I was ready to go for it. My friend walked up and struck

"Did you know?"

Those dark specks you see on the outer suns are not dust on my camera sensor, as one would think. They're sunspots, caused by concentrations of magnetic fields on the sun's surface. They can be more than ten times the size of the Earth!

The glowing halo around the total eclipse is called the corona – NOTHING to do with the virus! – which means "crown" in Spanish. In reference to the eclipse, the corona is the atmosphere of the sun, usually hidden by the brightness of the orb, and you can only see it during a total eclipse in the 100% totality zone.

up a conversation with the people in our area, trying to distract them and pull their attention away from me. But I swear, the few times I peeked around the bush, it looked like one of the guys was looking my way. Ew. Toni, you had better have been right that they couldn't see me. {Cringe.}

Moving on! Eclipse time finally approached, and it was more than we ever expected. The way the light changes before a total eclipse is just eerie, and oh-so-cool. You can see the odd darkness approaching from afar; this is when it would have been awesome to be at a higher viewing point. I would have loved to capture that unusual shadow covering part of the landscape. When the semi-shadow overtook us, the light got even weirder. In photographer's lingo, it was like having flat and high contrast light at the same time. The air seemed almost hazy when looking at each other, but it was still bright enough for us to cast shadows that were sharp and defined. Yet the shadows were not fully dark like you'd see in direct sunlight. Just... weird.

This experience was already soooo cool, and we hadn't even reached full eclipse yet!

I'd been shooting the partially blocked sun at intervals and was filled with an excitement unlike any other when the moment of total eclipse came. I captured the famed flare that gives the halo the look of a ring, and I captured the rare corona light around the sun that can only be seen during a total solar eclipse. I had to remind myself to also sit back and enjoy the experience with my own eyes, not just looking through my camera. It's easy to get caught up taking pictures and forget to enjoy the moment. But I enjoyed every second of the 2.5 minutes it took for the moon to pass between the sun and the earth.

My panoramic images are composites of the full 3 hour event, with totality lasting about 2.5 minutes. I look at my eclipse pictures and emotions override my thoughts as I recall that epic experience. It was one of the most amazing things I've ever seen, and I'll definitely be planning well ahead of time to reach the zone of totality and capture any solar eclipses I can in my lifetime.

◀ These nerds are ready for action!

Toni's wussy camera's view of the eclipse ▶

Photo by Antonia Kucera

◀ My fancy homemade solar filter

▲
◀ Ready to shoot!

Nature's Hidden Treasure A secret spot in Johnston Canyon (don't ask me where) – Banff National Park, Canada

October 2017

HOW DID I MISS THAT?

Banff National Park | Alberta, Canada

EXPOSURE
Shutter 10 sec. | Aperture f/11 | ISO 160

CAMERA GEAR
Nikon D810 | Nikkor 14-24 f/2.8 | Shot @ 14mm

october 2017

When my friend Toni and I first went to Banff in 2014, we were blown away by everything we saw. From glaciers and waterfalls to canyons and lakes, everything was truly magical. We fell in love with the Canadian Rocky Mountains, so much so that I would return three times over the next few years to keep exploring the multiple national parks.

The very first hike we ever did was Johnston Canyon, and it made an impression! The trail is very popular, and the park has built paved walkways that not only follow the top of the canyon, but actually take you along the canyon wall on walkways built into the cliffside! Without these walkways, it's difficult to see down into the steep canyon.

We spent 12 days exploring on that first trip, and I'd seen and captured so much that I was blissfully happy with my photos, even though I was sure there was more to see. If not for social media, I would have stayed happy as a clam! But one day on Instagram, I saw an amazing photo of a massive boulder with a glacial creek running around it… and it was tagged Johnston Canyon.

What the heck? How had I missed THAT? I was confused. We'd spent an entire day at Johnston Canyon, initially to get a waterfall shot **(See "How to Piss Off Tourists," page 50)**, but we also hiked the entire trail. We'd hit all the main viewpoints! After a bit of Googling, I found out this was a favorite local spot that's hard to see unless you're looking for it. I was certain I was going to find it next time.

Fast forward a year. I returned to Banff just before my annual park pass expired. Can't let that go to waste, right?

▲ Johnston Canyon, 2014

I scheduled myself a chunk of time exclusively to explore Johnston Canyon and find this mystery boulder. I awoke that morning energized – it was now or never, as I'd be heading north later that day. I headed to the trail early to avoid crowds, and so I could blur the water with a long exposure in the lower light. As I pulled into the parking lot, it seemed I would have the trail to myself!

But not for the reasons I thought. I geared up and headed to the trailhead to find it… closed. I was confused, to say the least, as this was peak tourist season. I went back to the gift shop and found out the trail was closed to clear out dead trees. I sensed there was more to the story and Googled the closure back at my hotel… only to find out a dead tree had fallen and killed a child! Oh… wow. I sat there, shocked and heartbroken for the family.

Needless to say, I didn't find the boulder that trip. It was a reminder that even on paved paths and man-made trails, nature is still wild and anything can happen.

A couple of years later, Toni and I were having Canada withdrawals. When a photo class with a photographer from Banff came up in October of 2017, we thought it was the perfect opportunity to see the park in a different season. We were excited to see the Larch Trees in all their glory, and I was excited at another opportunity to find that boulder. We visited the trail right away and I dragged my trusty travel buddy up the canyon at a fierce pace, certain that this time, I would find it!

I did not. Where the heck was this thing???

We went back to the hotel and I Googled furiously. Finding more information was difficult, but when I finally did, I understood why. It was more than just a favorite local spot,

EXPOSURE Shutter 1.6 sec. | Aperture f/16 | ISO 64   **CAMERA GEAR** Nikon D810 | Nikkor 28-70 f/2.8 | Shot @ 31mm

Hopeful Morning An early fall morning at Two Jack Lake, the day we finally found the secret spot – Banff National Park, Canada

October 2017

it was a secretive spot that the locals keep to themselves so it doesn't get overrun and ruined by high traffic... especially because you have to go off-trail to reach it.

Now I was torn. A few favorite local spots back home in the Black Hills had been ruined because their secretive locations were shared online **(see "Day of Discovery," page 100, for one example)**. But I wasn't here to destroy or disrespect nature – just the opposite! I wanted to preserve it through my photography.

I also don't normally go off-trail because the main pathways are there for a reason – to protect the area and to keep people safe. I decided we'd go look for the hidden spot one more time, and I could determine then if it's safe to venture off trail just this once. I wasn't ready to let it go yet. I just had to see this elusive place!

So we went again and walked the trail in the evening… and still, no luck! This boulder truly was hidden! Toni was exhausted from going up and down the trail, so she sat at a viewpoint while I tried and tried again. I was certain it had to be in this area… but I eventually slumped back to her, defeated. Toni always tries to keep me motivated on photo trips, and she said, "Maybe it's somewhere else on the trail? We've still got time to look." She waited while I went to look one last time.

Peering over an edge I hadn't looked down before, I saw something that was familiar… Excited, I ran back to Toni and said, "I think I found it!" We found some deer trails and, when we were alone on the trail, carefully followed them, doing our best to not disturb the fauna or loosen the ground on our way down to the water's edge.

And finally, I'd found it! It wasn't actually a boulder, but a piece of land that narrowed where the river carved around it, then widened at the bend so it only looked like a boulder in the photos I'd seen. I was able to photograph from the rocky ground without disturbing anything. While I was shooting, a local videographer and his friend showed up as well. They were also careful of their surroundings, and I think we were all appreciative that the people who had found this secret spot were respectful of its value.

This spot is difficult to find, and should probably remain that way. When someone wants to go off-trail – myself included – perhaps we should question not if we CAN, but if we SHOULD. (Hey, we learned that from a jurassic snafu too, thanks Dr. Ian!) Besides, with so much to enjoy in Johnston Canyon and the rest of Banff along the main trails, there's no need to take the road less traveled.

FINALLY!!! Showing off the scale of the "rock" with a selfie ▶

◀ Tired but smiling, searching over and over and over... ▶

BACK AND FORTH, BACK AND FORTH

Banff National Park | Alberta, Canada

EXPOSURE
Shutter 1/5 sec. | Aperture f/11 | ISO 100

CAMERA GEAR
Nikon D810 | Nikkor 14-24 f/2.8 | Shot @ 14mm

october 2017

When it comes to sunrise photos, I always try my best to plan ahead. Sunrise photos naturally require a little extra effort, as you're setting up in the dark. I usually visit the location beforehand and pick out my spot so I know exactly where to go when visibility is low. This helps reduce my anxiety of possibly choosing poorly in the morning, and it helps avoid panic attacks over missing the shot.

That didn't work out so well the morning of this shot.

This was the second time my friend Toni and I had gone to the Canadian Rockies together, and since we'd first gone in summer, we chose the fall for this trip to capture a different look. We started the trip in the Lake Louise area and lucked out with 70-degree sunshiny weather. We took advantage by hiking to see the Larch trees high up in the Valley of the Ten Peaks above Lake Moraine. It was stunning but felt a bit odd to be so far north in October and have balmy, sunny conditions.

Well, that all changed, and at the worst time!

I knew I wanted to shoot Herbert Lake for sunrise, so we needed to be up and out the door early. (Thankfully, not as early as in the summer!) I also already knew, from a previous visit to the lake, where I wanted to park and where to go to set up my shot. I was PREPARED!

After a good night's rest, we awoke to a dark, overcast sky. I knew that could change quickly from past experience, so we stuck to the plan and headed out. As we headed north from Lake Louise in the near-dark, the cloud cover got heavier and heavier and it seemed there would likely be no visible sunrise at Herbert Lake. But behind us, the clouds seemed to break up in the direction of Banff.

What to do, what to do…

We pressed on toward Herbert Lake, taking the exit for the Icefields Parkway. It got darker and darker… and then it started to snow! And not lightly - it was blowing sideways and was heavy enough that it was difficult to see the road. Plus our car didn't have four wheel drive.

We turned around and headed to Banff to shoot at Vermillion Lakes, one of my favorite spots in the area. From where we were it took over 30 minutes to drive down past Lake Louise to the town of Banff, and by this time we were encroaching on sunrise. We happened to look back to the north… and wouldn't you know, there was the lovely pink sky, back the direction we'd come from. Oh, the anxiety.

The light in Banff was blah and I sooo wanted the shot at Herbert Lake, so we turned around. Again. I wish I could just know where we had to be!

> "Sometimes you win, sometimes you don't."

We had to act fast. By the time we arrived back at Herbert Lake, the heavy clouds were gone… and so was the pink. Ugh. I was mad at myself for letting the fear of missing the perfect moment get the best of me. I wish we had just stuck it out, snowstorm and all, even if we couldn't yet see anything.

In the end, I'm still happy with the image I captured. The early morning light is still lovely, and the fresh snow on the ground echoes the snow on the mountains. It serves as a reminder to just pick a spot and see what happens. Sometimes you win, sometimes you don't, but you can't let the uncertainty of it all throw you off track. Because then, you're definitely going to miss out.

Elusive Winter Sun Our umpteenth visit of the morning (OK, I'm exaggerating...) to Herbert Lake – Banff National Park, Canada   October 2017

SOMETIMES THINGS GO SIDEWAYS

Port Campbell National Park | The Great Ocean Road, Australia

EXPOSURE	CAMERA GEAR
Shutter 1/200 sec.	Aperture f/7.1	ISO 800	Nikon D810	Nikkor 17-35 f/2.8	Shot @ 25mm

december 2017

At one point in my professional career, I decided to try and separate photography trips from vacations with family. Because it takes time to set up and photograph a scene, or to patiently seek a wild animal and carefully photograph it, I'd always feel bad when my husband or parents or whomever were left standing around waiting while I shoot.

But... sometimes you only get ONE opportunity to go somewhere. Traveling is expensive! Am I right?!

One such trip where I had to combine career with vacation was when I went to Australia with my niece in 2017. We'd planned the trip a while back as a celebration of her graduating high school and moving on to college, so I largely planned our days as a tourist would. However, I wasn't sure if or when I might have the chance to go to Australia again, so I brought all my professional gear along and tried to incorporate photo opportunities on our planned excursions.

In Melbourne we opted for a chauffeured tour of the Great Ocean Road – a trek that's considered one of the most beautiful drives in Australia. We could have rented a car, but the tour was scheduled to be at the famed Twelve Apostles for sunset. That was the light I was looking for, so guided tour it was!

There's a lot to see on this trek! We saw some amusingly tall trees (my niece and I are both short…), spotted some beautiful wild birds, and even saw a wild koala sleeping in a tree! It was such an amazing drive and we honestly could have spent days exploring the area. But we had a lot to pack in during our vacation, so we enjoyed these tourist-y moments with snapshots and I saved up my photographic time for the main attraction.

We arrived at the Twelve Apostles area early enough to do some exploring before hunkering down for sunset. The view definitely did not disappoint our tour group! But as a photographer who lives for that dramatic golden hour light, I was slightly bummed to see that I wasn't likely to get any amazing color. Regardless, I would get what I could!

Normally I like to do longer exposures to capture a scene, so I'd not only carried my fully loaded camera bag with me all day, but I'd lugged along a tripod. I really wanted a sharp image that would be beautiful as a fine art print, so I'd need to stabilize the tripod as much as possible. I'd also need to keep my ISO to 800 or less to avoid a grainy look. But even with all this effort, nature sadly doesn't always work with me. The WIND!!! It was soooooooooo windy!

Notice how the grass in this photo is going sideways?!?!

With 35 mph winds and full-on gusts even stronger than that, using a tripod was pointless. I had to crank up my exposure values WAY higher than I normally would, but this was my one and only chance and, dang it, I was going to create something memorable! I mean, I came all this way!

This photo may not be perfect when it comes to depth of field **(photo lingo – see tip on page 164)**, but the view is simply outstanding. And hey, at least the only thing that really went sideways were my epic sunset photo plans!

But this photo has something that's even more important: it encompasses wonderful memories of this special trip with my niece. And that's time well spent.

◀ Just a little breezy
▼ Road to adventure!

The Breezy Apostles Sideways blasting wind at the Twelve Apostles viewpoint off the The Great Ocean Road – Port Campbell National Park, Australia   December 2017

WORTH EVERY PENNY

Uluru-Kata Tjuta National Park | Northern Territory, Australia

EXPOSURE
Shutter 6 sec. | Aperture f/16 | ISO 200

CAMERA GEAR
Nikon D810 | Nikkor 28-70 f/2.8 | Shot @ 35mm

december
2017

As I sit and write about the main attraction I wanted to shoot in Australia, I'm realizing that most of the stories in this book are about what you can't see in the picture – particularly what I had to endure or accomplish to create the photo. This image of Uluru is the perfect example.

If you've read my Twelve Apostles story about the trip to Australia **(see previous page)**, you know that this special three-week adventure with my niece was both a vacation and a photography excursion. It was a challenge to pack – What would I reallllllly need? What's worth lugging along to the other side of the world? – and we also had a lot of sightseeing to cram in.

For example, we only had ONE day at the most iconic landmark in Australia: Ayers Rock, locally known as Uluru. I wish we'd had more time here; the Australian desert is so beautiful! Even though it was insanely hot. And full of giant bugs. And flies.

We arrived to our hotel near Ayers Rock on Christmas Eve in the balmy temp of 105 degrees Fahrenheit. Meanwhile, back home in South Dakota, it was five below zero. Even with the scary bugs, I was actually enjoying the dry heat. I mean, at least we had ice cream and air conditioning!

Ayers Rock Resort was such an interesting place! Ayers Rock itself is on aboriginal land, and the resort is the only tourist accommodation in the area. It's large enough and so far away from the cities that it has it's own airport! It was quite a large airport, all things considered, and it was great fun walking off the plane directly onto the tarmac. That doesn't happen much any more!

After our arrival we had the afternoon to explore the hotel grounds, and then we planned to rest up for our sunrise and sunset tours the next day. Smart people don't visit the rock past 9 or 10 am; the heat is just unbearable, and the FLIES! Did I mention the flies?

Let us talk about these little pests, for they are the reason I've included this story in my book. When we first arrived we checked out the gift shops (as all great tourists do) and we saw that they were selling head nets for $5. I thought for sure it must be a gimmick to make some extra cash off us gullible tourists. But just in case, I asked the sales clerk if the seemingly flimsy nets were really worth the cash. He told me in great confidence that we would most likely "find them useful."

Now, I've dealt with flies back home in the Black Hills, and sure, they're annoying, but I couldn't imagine actually needing nets to deal with flies. But hey, better to have them and not need them, so I dished out $10 to get the nets for my niece and me.

Best. Purchase. Ever.

Why? Because Australian flies are NOT normal!!!

New class: Official Outback Fashion 101

Enjoying the holidays down under

Sunburnt Uluru Ayers Rock, locally known as Uluru, minus the swarm of flies – Uluru-Kata Tjuta National Park, Australia

December 2017

These flies were definitely not from South Dakota. Wanna know why Australian flies are different? Oh, I learned. I learned the HARD way. You see, these flies like to ingest proteins and carbohydrates from human's tears and saliva. That means they land mostly around your eyes, nose and mouth to try and suck off your body fluids! Ewwwwww!

The flies were also so thick that after just a minute without the net, my hand was cramping from waving it around to keep the flies at bay! Needless to say we quickly got over feeling stupid for wearing such ugly headgear and donned the nets. Thankfully, they were plenty sturdy to keep the flies off our faces. (And really, I'm sure we looked much worse when we were frantically waving our hands in the air.)

Though having a blue net in my vision made it a challenge to compose my pictures, it was much worse before with flies trying to get in my MOUTH. Bleh. I'll take the lovely blue netting any day over that!

After all of that hassle, I was finally able to enjoy the moment. Watching the evening sun light up the orange rock of Uluru was truly a magical moment for me. By then, I didn't even notice the net.

THIS IS NOT A HAPPY PICTURE

Kakadu National Park | Darwin, Australia

EXPOSURE
Shutter 1/500 sec. | Aperture f/8 | ISO 400

CAMERA GEAR
Nikon D810 | Nikkor 28-70 f/2.8 | Shot @ 48mm

december 2017

Ah, yes... another seemingly innocent image that you would think evokes joy and happy memories! Sadly it only makes me think of one thing: puking.

Did I mention I get motion sick? Have all my life. Yet for some reason I thought it best to NOT take a motion sickness pill on a plane ride over the Australian outback. This was the trip I took with my niece after her first semester in college, and she politely refused a pill when I offered her one. So I didn't take one either.

Clouds Down Under Fluffy clouds that just make me sick – Kakadu National Park, Australia

December 2017

I am such an idiot. Even at 36 you can still make stupid choices! This was one of them.

We were on a two day tour of Kakadu National Park. Fun fact: this is where they filmed Crocodile Dundee! Our guide said the park is best viewed from the air since most of it is bushland, so we opted to splurge on the plane ride.

We arrived at the airport on a seemingly calm summer day, so I wasn't really concerned about turbulence – another factor in my ill-fated decision to skip motion sickness meds. The first problem came in the size and design of the plane: it was a small eight-seater, so I had to sit in the back and look out a side window. And yes, planes are just like cars for people who get motion sick – it's better to sit in front and look ahead so your eyes follow the motion, and it's terrible to look out the side and see everything rushing by.

The second problem was my determination to get a picture. You see, looking through the lens and zooming in and out DOUBLED the motion effect! Yep, it didn't take long before I was valiantly fighting nausea to keep taking pictures. Priorities, right?

It was so pretty and such a cool experience and I wanted so badly to enjoy it! But I finally hurled. Ugh. And to make matters worse, once my niece saw me get sick – not just once, but THREE times – she did too. I felt soooooo bad. Thankfully we kept it in the provided airbags though!

You would think that'd be the end of it, right? Wrong. Sooooo wrong. Oh yeah, there's MORE!

You see, Kakadu is full of really cool rock formations. When it's hot, these rock formations radiate heat and, guess what? Hot air pushes the plane up! So right when I thought the sickness might be over, the planed dropped. Then rose. Then dropped. You get the idea.

So a word to the wise for all those affected by motion sickness: a plane ride over rocky terrain on a hot day is just as bad as a boat cresting monster waves!

▲▲ Sneaky gator in the billabong
Ugh, you deceptive, rocky terrain! ▲
◄ So happy... poor naive tourists :(

After an hour of distress and beautiful scenery, we finally landed. I'd never been so happy to be on solid ground! I was so relieved… for about three seconds. We found out the next leg of our journey started just a short way down the road where we were going on a BOAT ride through a billabong (the fun word in Australia for a lake left after flood waters, or a pond left behind after a river changes course). Needless to say, the ride didn't go well.

And it was lunch time after all that, ha! I skipped the food and spent the lunch break sprawled out on a comfy sofa.

Maybe I'll eventually train my brain to look at these fluffy clouds and think of that fluffy sofa… not the misery that came before!

I hope so, because I really do love this image.

THE PHOTO THAT COST A FORTUNE
Royal Botanical Gardens in Sydney | New South Wales, Australia

EXPOSURE
Shutter 15 sec. | Aperture f/18 | ISO 200

CAMERA GEAR
Nikon D810 | Nikkor 28-70 f/2.8 | Shot @ 62mm

december 2017

This photo represents a pretty cool moment for me – I got to be one of the first people on the planet to celebrate and ring in the New Year. Now, let me tell you why this is the most expensive single image, to date, that I've ever created.

When planning our big Australia trip, it didn't even cross my mind to look for a fireworks event, even though we'd be in Australia on New Year's Eve. My travel agent was actually the one to realize this, and she arranged a stop that would take us to Sydney right in time for the biggest display in the country.

I had to do more coordinating and had to spend more money on access for this photo than any other before it, which is crazy. I found out that the best place to view the display would be from the Royal Botanical Gardens, and you had to first be a member to be able to get the worthwhile tickets for the show: members get first pick at the tickets. I got a peek at the layouts and views for each "party zone" they designated for the event. Of course, the zone with the best view was the most expensive.

Rather than wasting my day sitting on my butt, camping out somewhere in the city for a chance at a view, I bit the bullet and bought the Royal Botanical Garden tickets for my niece and myself.

I can't quite remember the exact cost of the tickets, but compared to any other event I'd ever been to, the price was astronomical. Figure in the cost of the trip overall – flights, hotel, food – and yeah, this is one pricey photo!

A quick WTF moment here... earlier in the trip I'd met a super fun family at Uluru (hundreds of miles away from Sydney), and after chatting for a while as we swatted at flies, I took their family Christmas photo for them. Well, imagine my surprise to run into the same family in Sydney earlier that day! Random, but how cool?

The city of Sydney basically shuts down for the New Year's Eve party, and they do their best to make sure people are safe. Still, it was nice to not have to fight the crowds, and we felt like we had VIP status when we arrived at the party and got our fancy box dinners at our reserved table. We kinda ate our food – some of it was really weird! So… worth the money yet? Not quite.

Back to the event! I realized early on that I couldn't shoot from our table – there would be too many people in the way. Not only that, but when the party picked up, people started making their way to the rock wall by the water. Oh no! I was NOT going to have my camera blocked after all this. So well before the practice fireworks started at 9 pm, I hauled my gear to the waterfront and claimed my spot.

▲ Enjoying checking the Sydney Opera House off my bucket list

Parked at the gardens... I'm not moving! ▲

New Year of Fortune A pricey view of New Year's Eve Fireworks above the Sydney Opera House – Australia

December 2017

If only I'd known the people who owned those boats…

After the first round of fireworks, my niece came over, looked at me head on, and asked, "Do you really plan to stand there all the way until midnight???"

I looked her dead in the eye and said, "Yes. Yes I do." After everything I did to get there, I was NOT giving up my spot! (Hey, that's the only time I left her hanging in our three weeks together!)

Crazy thing is that after everything, I almost, ALMOST didn't get my shot. One particular boat in the harbor was just smack dab in the front and center of everything, totally messing up the composition. Thankfully the boat slowly puttered out of my frame and I finally nailed this shot of the iconic Sydney Opera House wrapped in glowing light and bright fireworks.

Now was it worth the money? Absolutely.

THE BADGER BABES

Grand Teton National Park | Wyoming, United States

EXPOSURE **CAMERA GEAR**
Shutter 1/640 sec. | Aperture f/8 | ISO 800   Nikon D610 | Nikkor 300 f/2.8 | 420mm w/ Nikkor TC -14E II

2018 may

I have seen many critters in my life, but until 2018 I'd only ever had a few brief encounters with one of the most elusive and majestic of small animals: the badger. My first encounter barely counts – I nearly tripped on one in the dark during a 1998 high school art trip to Yellowstone! I can still see those glowing eyes and hear that scary hiss, and it brings to mind every wildlife show I've ever seen that warns against approaching these often aggressive creatures.

Still, I wanted to see one! And as my luck would have it, my dry spell was about to end on a beautiful day spent in the Tetons with two of my good friends.

I've had so many wonderful photography trips in the Tetons that any time I can swing the cost, I have to go! **(See stories on pages 42-45 and 56-61, for starters.)** I came home with so many awesome images that I started taking other photographers, like the trip in 2017 when a friend and I saw grizzly bears! **(See "Bear-ly Holding On," page 108)**.

Fast forward to 2018. I had planned to teach a workshop in one of my favorite national parks and decided on the Tetons, hoping to share with others the wondrous things I had seen these last few years. I ran into insurance issues and had to cancel, but my friend Deb and her sister Jan still wanted to go, so bam! Off I went to the Tetons again!

I LOVED showing them all of my favorite places. We lucked out and had a couple of great sunrises and one stellar sunset. Overall we simply enjoyed each other's company and went where the winds would take us! We even ventured off the beaten path to see what treasures might be lurking in the woods. One of these treasures, the badger, was a first for all of us.

We'd pulled over, parked and walked in to explore some old homestead ruins, and Jan suddenly let out a scream! Startled, Deb and I turned to her, and she yelled to us, "It's a badger!" She said some movement in her peripheral vision had caught her eye, and there it was! I'm sure the looks on our faces exuded disbelief, but it was, indeed, a badger. Our excited approach startled it, however, and it took off.

We were bummed not to have any pictures to prove our amazing encounter, but we were still elated to have seen one of nature's more elusive critters.

So back to exploring we went! We wandered around for a good twenty minutes, giving this piece of history the respect it deserves. Any time I see these homesteads, all I can think about is if I could have handled living like they did back in the day. So far from civilization, alone in the woods and days from help… I've concluded every time that I likely would have died of dysentery or one of the other dreadful downfalls from the Oregon Trail! But all the beautiful fresh mountain air might be worth the risk.

I was exploring the area and pondering these thoughts when we grouped together again

Photo by Deb Zimmerman

◀◀◀ Cool rustic cabin window view
◀◀ Deb's picture of our little badger friend
◀ A portrait view of our handsome badger buddy

Whatchu Lookin' At? Our friend the badger peeking up from his dirt shower – Grand Teton National Park, USA

May 2018

by the cabin… and stopped in surprise. What the… our friend the badger had returned and was diligently digging a hole!

From what I have seen on nature shows, badgers are not to be messed with, and with my Yellowstone encounter the only experience the three of us had to look back on, we quickly piled into the cabin for safety, peeking out a window at the mysterious creature. Ha, I can only imagine how we must have looked to the badger!

Of course, we were NOT prepared with proper zoom lenses to capture wildlife. Deb and I were both cursing under our breaths at not having our bags with us. But as the badger continued to dig and dig… I concluded he was distracted enough that I could sneak out to the car for our lenses. I slowly exited the cabin, walking calmly to the car… and the badger barely noticed me! In truth, he only seemed interested in his hole, getting dirt and burrs and all sorts of ground material all over himself. I was able to get to the car and grab our big lenses without disturbing him in any way.

Jan joined me outside and crept to the corner of the cabin to start shooting. I ended up getting a little closer and sitting down in the grass some 20 feet from the badger and his little project. He didn't seem to mind me or my friends in the slightest. I sensed no anger from it – only curiosity.

In high school I had read a book by wilderness guru Tom Brown, a story of how he had befriended a badger. Such an idea was so beautiful to me, and sitting here provided a glimpse of what such a friendship might have been like. It was so peaceful and quiet – other than the click of our shutters, of course – but it was a moment I'll never forget.

We must have spent an hour with the little guy, clicking away between grins at each other. I shot close-ups of the badger from my spot in the grass and Deb captured a landscape with the Teton range in the background from her vantage point through the cabin window. It was just… magical.

Eventually the badger decided the hole was deep enough and took off, I'm assuming to where it's den might be. Satisfied, we packed up our gear and headed back to town. We proudly proclaimed ourselves The Badger Babes for the rest of the trip, and we even found fun mugs with a badger on them to commemorate our adventure.

The better keepsake, however, are the pictures themselves – they will always remind me of that wondrous feeling of being in harmony with nature.

See Ma? I Eat My Veggies! A rambunctious brown bear toddler showing off his grass grazing skills – Lake Clark National Park, USA

July 2018

WORTH THE COST?

Lake Clark National Park | Alaska, United States

EXPOSURE
Shutter 1/250 sec. | Aperture f/4 | ISO 800

CAMERA GEAR
Nikon D610 | Nikkor 70-200 f/2.8 | Shot @ 190mm

2018 july

I had been to Alaska a few times on cruises before 2018 and had, at some point, heard about the secluded brown bears in the little-known Lake Clark National Park. I'd only ever photographed bears from the safety of my car, and I yearned for the opportunity to safely capture them in the wild. But after seeing the cost of the stay at the lodge, my hopes were dashed. I just couldn't justify investing the money involved at the time.

But as I've gotten older, I think of my grandparents and their travels more and more. I knew I would regret any opportunities that I didn't take advantage of. So when my husband said he wanted to save up for another Alaskan cruise, we thought to invite my friend Toni along to share our favorite parts of Alaska – and to share some travel costs. I finally decided I was going to photograph the bears at Lake Clark. I didn't care what it would cost!

I was actually feeling pretty good about the cost of our trip when we found several great deals on accommodations, and splitting costs was so much better than when my husband and I had traveled alone! But I started to feel guilty about costs again when I figured in my bear adventure. The plan was for me to go up first and stay at Lake Clark for several days, then join my husband and friend when they flew in to start our vacation together. Compared to everything, my stay with the bears would be the most expensive part of the trip, and going solo on that part meant there was no help with sharing the cost. In fact, Lake Clark is, as of 2020, the most expensive photo venture I've ever had on a cost-per-day basis.

I was steeped in buyer's remorse on the whole flight to Alaska. I got myself so stressed out about the money that when I arrived at the airport in Anchorage, I left my tripod in a locker in my other bag (I stored a separate bag for the cruise) and had to go back for it! Not a good start.

The stressful mood held and I nearly had an anxiety attack the next morning when I arrived at the little local airport and saw the tiny plane that would take me to the lodge. My last ride on a small plane hadn't gone well **(see "This is Not a Happy Picture" on page 124)**. I nervously waited by a little plane with buoys on the front, both excited and trepidatious about landing on water.

As I waited for the pilot, a helpful little voice in my head went on and on about how there was no way photos of bears were going to be worth the cost. I have never in my life been so glad for that little voice to be so wrong!

Every part of the trip from then on was incredible. I was actually by the wrong plane – we would NOT be landing in the sea – and I followed the pilot to a wheeled plane named The Beaver. Landing on the secluded beach was an awesome experience, so thrilling! We'd flown over breath-taking green landscapes next to ocean inlets, and since I'd wisely taken motion sickness meds and asked to sit up front, I got to take pics. Even the ride on the ATV to the lodge was fun, especially when, on the way, I already saw a

Beach landing in "The Beaver" ▼

bear! Seeing a bear so soon erased all of my doubts. This trip was totally going to be worth the cost.

I spent the next several days in brown bear heaven! We woke up at the crack of dawn every day to go look for bears, came back to the lodge for breakfast, then went right back out for more bears. We'd stay out until lunch time, or occasionally come back early to greet newcomers who had flown in. We got to relax after lunch and had time to shower if needed before taking off again mid-afternoon. More bears! The dinner bell would ring at 6, and then – you guessed it – we'd head right back out and stay out until the park closed or weather drove us inside.

And it would take extreme weather to keep us inside! The schedule held, rain or shine. My first few days in the park were crazy warm, with temperatures upward of 90 degrees! Not what I expected in Alaska, but the rest of the weather was. The remaining days were cold with solid, unrelenting rain. We had to hang our clothes by the fire to dry them while we ate. I'd thankfully packed well for the trip, and my gear kept me warm and dry and my camera protected. Plus the bears looked so cool in the rain that I didn't even care about the sun disappearing! (That's unusual for me.) The trip was also made enjoyable by the new friends I made on our excursions. I spent much of the time bouncing around in the ATV trailers with some older gentlemen, two of which were friends who travel together as much as they can. We all hit it off, and I highly enjoyed their antics and friendly teasing. Truly, the company on an adventure can make or break the experience!

I loved every minute of my trip. I'd wake up to bears outside my window almost every day! Normally that might be terrifying, but there's a unique situation with the bears in Lake Clark.

> "Life is too short to wait for 'Someday' to happen."

You see, hunting is not allowed and the land is protected, so without being threatened by the humans in residence, the bears don't feel the need to chase or scare off the photographers. We could be in a field just 30 feet away from a mama bear and her cubs, and everyone, bears included, were safe. Don't get me wrong, we were still cautious – a couple of bears wandered into the lodge area one day, and everyone stayed inside or kept at least a car between them and the animals, respecting their right to be there.

The most harrowing things got was when curious baby bears tried to eat the tour guide's ATV! We'd spotted the bear family in a field and walked in to set up for photos. Meanwhile the curious cubs circled around for their snack, and the guide had to shoosh them away!

The baby cubs were a favorite, of course. Their antics, whether chomping down green grass in a rainy field or digging for clams on the beach, were adorable. And sometimes it seemed like the bears were intentionally giving us a show! One day our ATV ride halted as a juvenile male bear lumbered out of the brush near the path. I'd happened to put my camera away, so I didn't join in on the shutter-fest when the big bear found a tree and stood up to use it as a back-scratch pole! I just sat and happily enjoyed the experience. I swear, that bear kept looking over to make sure people were still taking pictures of him! It was so joyful!

This trip will forever be etched in my brain in its entirety. If I'd had the money, I would have booked a return trip right then and there! I actually met a few guys who go back every year (I have no idea how they afford it, but I'm jealous). I'll have to settle for saving up for a time when I can afford to go again, because this haven is definitely worth the cost.

My experience with the bears just solidifies one of my life views: don't wait to take that trip, or whatever you may be putting off... DO IT as soon as you can. Life is too short to wait for "Someday" to happen.

◀ Getting up close & personal with bears!

EXPOSURE Shutter 1/2000 sec. | Aperture f/7.1 | ISO 400   **CAMERA GEAR** Nikon D810 | Nikkor 300 f/2.8 | Shot @ 420mm w/ Nikkor TC-14E II

Gettin' Clams for Mom's Chowder An Alaskan Brown Bear diligently digging for clams on a protected beach – Lake Clark National Park, USA

DINNER IS SERVED

Protected Waters of Annette Island | Alaska, United States

EXPOSURE
Shutter 1/4000 sec. | Aperture f/7.1 | ISO 400

CAMERA GEAR
Nikon D810 | Nikkor 300 f/2.8

2018 *july*

Though this shot was taken in 2018, it actually began in 2015 when my husband and I went on our first Alaskan cruise together. Since I was on vacation and didn't expect to have any opportunities to take award winning photos from a cruise ship, I only brought along a "travel lens." This means the lens is handy for fun vacation shots, but it's lacking in the professional department – it's not super fast, meaning it's slow to focus when following movement, and it has lower quality, less expensive glass, meaning the images are not as sharp as ones from my more expensive, higher quality lenses.

This travel lens was perfect for the excursions my husband and I chose in Ketchikan. The big treat for the day was to go out on the Aleutian Ballad, one of the original crab fishing boats from Discovery's Deadliest Catch series. The boat was a bit smaller than we realized, but still cool to see! As big fans of the show, we were enthralled to meet the likes of David Lethin and Andy Pittard (Andy is highly entertaining, btw), and see up close the skills of a crab fisherman.

During the demonstration of longline fishing, the crew chops up bait fish; I remember thinking "That's a lot of fish… I hope it doesn't go to waste!" Shortly after, the crew announced they had a special treat in store for us and we angled toward the nearest shoreline.

All of a sudden, the sky was filled with bald eagles!

So you can imagine my disappointment to be holding a crappy lens while being surrounded by these amazing eagles, diving and soaring and fighting over the bait fish the crew tossed to them. There were eagles EVERYWHERE, more than I'd seen in my life! And I walked away with ZERO photographs that day. It was an amazing experience, but the photographer in me was crushed.

Fast forward to the summer of 2018 when opportunity knocked in the form of a friend, Toni, who had never been on an Alaskan cruise. My husband and I were ready for a getaway and we enjoy sharing experiences with friends, so we happily took Toni along on the same Alaskan cruise route.

◀ Alaska travel adventures!

Rise Above It Eagles galore!!! Seen on an excursion into the protected waters of Annette Island – Alaska, USA

July 2018

I was beyond excited for the Ketchikan stop! My husband chose to do a salmon fishing excursion for a new experience that day, but I was excited to repeat the crab tour with Toni, just for the "15 minutes of eagle ecstasy," as I called it.

Determined to get up close and personal with the eagles through my lens, I boarded the boat with my 300 mm f2.8 monster lens mounted and hurried to grab a seat close to the edge so I could beat the crowd to a good viewing spot.

As tourists walked by me on the boat I got many confused looks – they could not seem to fathom why I had such a gigantic lens on this tour. They didn't know about the eagles, of course. I chose to share the upcoming amazing surprise with those seated near us, but I think overall most of the tourists on the boat thought I was crazy!

Tourist stares aside, I was so excited to finally get some awesome photos of these eagles!

Once we finally arrived at the eagle spectacle, I jumped to the edge, hefted my lens up and looked through my viewfinder… oh no.

Would you believe that this time I loaded too LARGE of a lens for photographing the eagles?!?! The lens got me so close to the eagles that they over-filled the frame. I had hoped with the 300 mm to capture some pretty close images, but not THAT close! I would've been better off with my 70-200 mm lens for this exact instance, but once the eagles were flying there just wasn't time to switch lenses.

Most of my shots did not work, but I was thankfully able to capture a few stunning images, the above being one of them. This one shot and the experience of having countless eagles dancing in the air around me was absolutely worth the second visit. Perhaps opportunity will knock again and I'll have that 70-200 ready to shoot!

EXPECT THE UNEXPECTED

Custer State Park | South Dakota, United States

EXPOSURE
Shutter 1.3 sec. | Aperture f/9 | ISO 200

CAMERA GEAR
Nikon D810 | Nikkor 14-24 f/2.8 | Shot @ 22mm

2019 june

Sylvan Lake is a gorgeous spot just an hour's drive from where I live, and yet after years of early morning and late day attempts, an epic sunrise or sunset picture eluded me. I'd leave Rapid City with promising skies, only to arrive at Sylvan to find dull overcast light or nearly impenetrable fog. So you can imagine my surprise when THIS sunset happened while I was teaching a class.

We need to rewind though, as the whole day deserves merit. The plan was to meet at my house in the afternoon for some education and camera review, then head to a location with a cool rustic building to learn how to work the scene, and end the day at Sylvan to work on landscape composition and exposing for golden hour light.

I was out running errands earlier in the day, and I started to get concerned as the craziest storm seemed to come out of nowhere! We rushed home to find the streets flooded and piles of hail so deep, they looked like snow. I was particularly concerned for one student driving up from Hot Springs, as the storm was headed her direction. I texted her a warning and was glad when she arrived safely.

Luckily the heavy part of the storm passed quickly, so we could forge ahead with the class! We had fun at the first location, even though we got rained on a little. I like to be hands-on with my students, mainly using my own camera for demonstration and working with each student to help them learn to first compose a scene in their head, then frame it up with their own camera.

With the stormy weather so far, I was feeling like I'd once again find a gloomy scene at Sylvan. But to my delight, I noticed some white highlights in the clouds when we arrived. Maybe we'd be in for something special!

We started at the Black Elk Peak trailhead and worked our way towards the back of the lake, having fun exploring the unique area and the ever-changing light. Black Hills weather can change in a matter of minutes, so you have to run with what it gives you.

We reached a spot I determined would be perfect for sunset, and I instructed the students to watch as I set up my tripod and camera in preparation. After a talk about what to be aware of for a sunset exposure, my students started setting up with their equipment. This was going to be tricky! Everyone's set-up was different, there weren't enough filters for everyone so they'd have to share, and if we got any color it could be over quickly.

Now, I normally take very few pictures when I'm teaching, but as the most colorful, fiery sunset I've ever seen in the Black Hills started to ignite in front of me, I couldn't resist. And hey, I'm an excellent multi-tasker! I spent most of the sunset running back and forth between the students and my camera, clicking a few pics for myself before zipping off to help someone in need. The whole time I reminded everyone to enjoy the sunset with their own eyes, not just through their cameras. I did the same as I moved about, and I'm lucky I didn't trip on anything. I was sooooooo focused on that sky!

As the minutes ticked by the light became more and more orange and then pink… and it seemed like the whole sky was on fire. It was completely unlike anything I had seen in the Black Hills before, and I was so glad we got to share the experience. We all walked away with beautiful images, happy memories, and some budding new friendships built on this amazing shared experience. Class dismissed!

Burned Into Memory The most amazing sunset EVER at Sylvan Lake – Black Hills National Forest of South Dakota, USA

June 2019

DON'T WAIT FOR RETIREMENT

Northern Rocky Mountains | Colorado, United States

EXPOSURE
Shutter 1/3200 sec. | Aperture f/5 | ISO 500

CAMERA GEAR
Nikon D810 | Nikkor 300 f/2.8 | 420mm w/ Nikkor TC -14E II

2019 — august

I have always dreamed of photographing a bull moose in the water! They happen to be my favorite animal, and I was in heaven in 2017 when I got to see 20 moose all in one day. But still, no epic water shot. Knowing this, a friend of mine invited me to go on a "Moose Weekend" event he was hosting for friends who, like me, wanted to see moose. He wanted to take us out to see these amazing animals in The Rockies, so of course, I quickly replied with a resounding "YES!"

The drive from the Black Hills to Colorado went smoothly. I arrived at about 3pm, and we didn't waste time getting the tour going! As soon as the whole group congregated, we packed ourselves and our gear up in the tour vehicles and headed out to find moose.

And wouldn't you know, we found moose in a pond on our first drive! Since my friend knew that was exactly what I'd hoped for, I joked that I could go home tomorrow! Turns out, I may as well have.

We had a pretty mixed group, from younger photographers like me to an elderly retired couple just wanting to take in the sights. On the hike to the pond with the moose, it became pretty evident that our group had a range of health issues, and I noticed at the pond that the elderly couple wasn't there with us. They did eventually get there, but the wife wasn't doing so well. It took a group effort for all of us to get her back to the car, and thankfully we were all able to stay calm and not add to the poor woman's anxiety. I was grateful to have gotten my Wilderness First Responder training after a worse experience on a trail **(see "Temperamental Ice," page 66)**, as it helped me to stay calm and assist when needed. I was proud to keep a cool head, thankful that no moose charged us, and glad when we made it back to the vehicles safely.

This all took longer than planned for that spot, so we decided to head back to the cabin and start fresh in the morning. I hoped the lady would be more up to the planned activities the next day. Don't get me wrong, I have no ill feelings toward her – I know she felt terrible about slowing us down and causing everyone to worry. I felt so bad that this lady finally got to pursue the dream of an experience she wanted to have, only to be derailed by her failing health.

It's one of the reasons that when anyone tells me they'll go on that trip, or do this or get to that "someday," I always think of something I heard in a movie: "'Someday' is really just code for never." And to that I say, "If you can, do it NOW."

> **"'Someday' is really just code for never... If you can, do it NOW."**

The couple stayed behind to rest the next morning while the rest of us went out to shoot. When we returned for lunch the lady seemed to be feeling much better, so we all packed up and once again headed out. Our first stop that afternoon was a short walk from a rest area to a field of flowers. The lady, apparently nervous after the previous day, opted to stay with the vehicles. Since I didn't have a macro lens, I hung back as well. But her husband started down the trail with the rest of the group.

Shortly after leaving, the husband returned for a different lens, then headed right back down the trail. The group returned after an hour… but the husband was not among them.

Huh… we all figured he must have gotten distracted and gone off trail somewhere. We looked around a bit with no luck, and figuring he'd be back soon, we waited. Twenty minutes passed. Then forty. After an hour, we got worried.

Tall Drink of Water My dream shot of a moose in water! – Rocky Mountains of Colorado, USA

August 2019

There was no cell reception where we were, but our host knew there was an emergency-use "mountain phone" just a few miles down the road. He took one carload to call in search and rescue, while the rest of us waited in case the lost man returned. It took quite a while for them to return from the call – the phone hadn't had the best signal. But they finally got a call to go through, and help would be coming!

As you can imagine, the wife was quite frantic. Heck, who wouldn't be worried about an elderly man being lost in the mountains? Anything could happen! I hate to say it, but by this time I was thinking, "What the heck are you two doing going on a trip like this?!?" I mean, if anything they could have found a tour made for seniors and enjoyed seeing moose safely, instead of putting their friend in this situation.

Some two hours later the man finally showed up, but the drama train was already rolling. We made the trip back to the emergency phone, but this time the signal wouldn't go through at all. There was no way to call off search and rescue before resources went to waste.

Needless to say, the last 24 hours had just been a horrible mess overall. My friend ended up having a discussion with the couple and told them that for liability reasons, he couldn't allow them to stay and take part in the outings. They left, but apparently didn't learn much of anything from their misadventures! We ran into them driving in a risky area on their own the next day. (Sigh…)

The whole experience solidified my thoughts on life. You can't predict the future or your health, so start saving NOW and MAKE time to do the things that bring you joy. Why wait? What if when you retire, you're no longer able to afford your dreams, or what if you're not able to do them physically? Don't wait for retirement. Live for the now.

School's Out Forever The star pupil at an abandoned schoolhouse, somewhere by Bear Butte – Near Sturgis, South Dakota, USA

August 2019

TAKING ANOTHER LOOK

Bear Butte Area | South Dakota, United States

EXPOSURE
Shutter 1/30 sec. | Aperture f/8 | ISO 320

CAMERA GEAR
Nikon Z7 | Nikkor 28-70mm f/2.8 | Shot @ 28mm

august 2019

I've gotten to know quite a few other photographers over the years, both locally and around the world. And we TALK, I tell ya! We share our photos and chat about our exposure and equipment, and when we're really feeling the camaraderie we'll share the locations of our favorite hidden spots.

Not that you can always find them, even with directions!

One local friend had told me about this amazing abandoned old schoolhouse they'd found in a field full of horses, somewhere by Bear Butte. Now I had already been allllll over the Bear Butte area **(see the "Crap, Which Road Was It?" story on page 88)**, and I had never seen an old schoolhouse, or horses for that matter! Still, I looked again. And still, no schoolhouse.

When my photographer friend Mike came to visit from Boston, I thought we could keep an eye out for the schoolhouse together while I showed him my favorite shooting spots in the Black Hills. Heck, why not explore some new roads? Who knows what we might find?!

I truly had a blast showing my friend around the Bear Butte area. Being a big city boy, he'd never seen such wide-open spaces before, especially with such unusual features as Bear Butte sticking up out of the terrain. He was simply going "bananas" (his words) and his enthusiasm was contagious. I was getting to see my home through a new pair of eyes, and I appreciated the refreshing viewpoint.

Those of us who live in the Black Hills area likely often hear that we "take it for granted," and that's usually true for anyone living in a scenic area. When you see it every day, you get less and less excited about it. Seeing my big city friend get so amped up over my home was a great reminder of how lucky I am to live here.

And to make the day even more exciting, we found the schoolhouse!!! Don't ask me where though, I'm still not sure which road it's on and I'd have to wander to find it again!

> **"Then the MAGIC happened."**

When we found the cool rustic building, we were lucky with the light as well. It was bright enough for shooting and there were enough clouds to soften the light. The schoolhouse was partially on private land, so we worked the scene and did our best to photograph without trespassing. As I worked my way to a front view of the building, I thought about the horses my local friend had mentioned. I was bummed they weren't around – my Boston city-born-and-bred friend would have gotten a big kick out of that!

I was snapping a few straight-on shots when the "blanket" I saw hanging inside the doorway went ~swish~...

Wait, what??? Did that just move? What did I just see?

Next thing I knew a horse's butt appeared in the doorway, followed by a tail. I barely held in an excited squeal and struggled to keep myself from jumping up and down. I did the not-so-subtle whisper-yell thing to Mike, waving him over and saying, "Hurry up, get over here!"

Then the magic happened. The horse awkwardly turned around... and stood with his head sticking right out of the doorway. He stood like that for quite some time! It was so comical and beautiful.

Eventually he exited, followed by TWO other horse buddies that were hidden inside the schoolhouse. Well, that's it I thought... school's out.

BONUS: 2020 WAS A BLAST, RIGHT?!?!

Mount Rushmore National Memorial | South Dakota, United States

EXPOSURE
Shutter 6 sec. | Aperture f/14 | ISO 80

CAMERA GEAR
Nikon D810 | Nikkor 70-200 f/2.8 | Shot @ 195mm

july 2020

What better way for a local Black Hills photographer to wrap up her book than with an epic Mount Rushmore fireworks photo from the crazy year when we actually managed to finish this fun project?

Having lived in the beautiful Black Hills of South Dakota most of my life, I was fortunate to be able to see the 4th of July fireworks at Mount Rushmore National Memorial multiple times, even though the event took a decade long hiatus in 2009 (largely due to fire danger). So when the 2020 event was announced, I got excited to photograph the fireworks once again!

Thinking back… I could only remember photographing the fireworks once! What?!?! That can't be right… but a glance back through old files and film produced just a couple pages of Velvia 50 slide film. They were from back in 2001, taken while on a visit home during my college years.

Back then, the 4th of July fireworks display at the monument was a first come, first serve event, save for a small section at the amphitheater with reserved seating. My grandfather had thoughtfully purchased a couple of seats, and he was kind enough to give me his tickets so I could photograph the event for the first time.

The 2001 tickets did NOT, however, include a reserved parking spot! I took my boyfriend at the time and we had to walk up almost the entire hill out of Keystone, the tourist town a few miles below Mount Rushmore. It was a climb! But it was a good thing afterwards – traffic was so backed up leaving the memorial that we were walking faster than the cars were moving.

▲ The smoky & colorful 2001 fireworks display

Seriously, we passed cars on foot! The trek was well worth the experience though, and I was excited to see what I had captured.

As you can guess, 20 years ago I thought my images were amazing. Digital era photographers will never know the stress of shooting slide film… your exposure has to be spot-on, but the color you get when you do it right is sooooo pretty. I love how the old bulbs they used to light Mount Rushmore gave the rocks a green cast while the bulbs warmed up, and how it complemented the bright colors of the fireworks. Such a unique look!

But to give some perspective: out of about 72 shots from that night, I ended up with only 2-3 images I liked. I knew I had to get out there for the 2020 display and capture this momentous event with my new gear. What difference does 20 years make? Well for one thing, out of about 85 shots taken, I ended up with 55 shots that I liked. Talk about an advancement in my skills! Yeah! (It's always nice to see your hard work pay off.)

I was so happy to have more "keepers" in 2020, and not just as proof of my personal growth. Why else, you ask? Well, how about needing positive results after 10 HOURS of sweltering in 90 degree heat!

Before I dive into all the "What the f?" moments in this story, let's address the elephant in the room. The year 2020 is rife with politics, protests and a global pandemic. I do not plan to touch base on any of those topics, or my thoughts on things one way or another, during the telling of this story. This book was largely written for laughs, smiles, and inspiration, and the hot topics of 2020 are widely discussed in plenty of other places.

And yes, this story definitely has enough "What the f?" moments on it's own without the additional craziness of the year 2020!

TAKING ANOTHER LOOK

Bear Butte Area | South Dakota, United States

EXPOSURE	CAMERA GEAR
Shutter 1/30 sec.	Aperture f/8	ISO 320	Nikon Z7	Nikkor 28-70mm f/2.8	Shot @ 28mm

august 2019

I've gotten to know quite a few other photographers over the years, both locally and around the world. And we TALK, I tell ya! We share our photos and chat about our exposure and equipment, and when we're really feeling the camaraderie we'll share the locations of our favorite hidden spots.

Not that you can always find them, even with directions!

One local friend had told me about this amazing abandoned old schoolhouse they'd found in a field full of horses, somewhere by Bear Butte. Now I had already been allllll over the Bear Butte area **(see the "Crap, Which Road Was It?" story on page 88)**, and I had never seen an old schoolhouse, or horses for that matter! Still, I looked again. And still, no schoolhouse.

When my photographer friend Mike came to visit from Boston, I thought we could keep an eye out for the schoolhouse together while I showed him my favorite shooting spots in the Black Hills. Heck, why not explore some new roads? Who knows what we might find?!

I truly had a blast showing my friend around the Bear Butte area. Being a big city boy, he'd never seen such wide-open spaces before, especially with such unusual features as Bear Butte sticking up out of the terrain. He was simply going "bananas" (his words) and his enthusiasm was contagious. I was getting to see my home through a new pair of eyes, and I appreciated the refreshing viewpoint.

Those of us who live in the Black Hills area likely often hear that we "take it for granted," and that's usually true for anyone living in a scenic area. When you see it every day, you get less and less excited about it. Seeing my big city friend get so amped up over my home was a great reminder of how lucky I am to live here.

And to make the day even more exciting, we found the schoolhouse!!! Don't ask me where though, I'm still not sure which road it's on and I'd have to wander to find it again!

> "Then the MAGIC happened."

When we found the cool rustic building, we were lucky with the light as well. It was bright enough for shooting and there were enough clouds to soften the light. The schoolhouse was partially on private land, so we worked the scene and did our best to photograph without trespassing. As I worked my way to a front view of the building, I thought about the horses my local friend had mentioned. I was bummed they weren't around – my Boston city-born-and-bred friend would have gotten a big kick out of that!

I was snapping a few straight-on shots when the "blanket" I saw hanging inside the doorway went ~swish~...

Wait, what??? Did that just move? What did I just see?

Next thing I knew a horse's butt appeared in the doorway, followed by a tail. I barely held in an excited squeal and struggled to keep myself from jumping up and down. I did the not-so-subtle whisper-yell thing to Mike, waving him over and saying, "Hurry up, get over here!"

Then the magic happened. The horse awkwardly turned around... and stood with his head sticking right out of the doorway. He stood like that for quite some time! It was so comical and beautiful.

Eventually he exited, followed by TWO other horse buddies that were hidden inside the schoolhouse. Well, that's it I thought… school's out.

BONUS: 2020 WAS A BLAST, RIGHT?!?!

Mount Rushmore National Memorial | South Dakota, United States

EXPOSURE
Shutter 6 sec. | Aperture f/14 | ISO 80

CAMERA GEAR
Nikon D810 | Nikkor 70-200 f/2.8 | Shot @ 195mm

2020 july

What better way for a local Black Hills photographer to wrap up her book than with an epic Mount Rushmore fireworks photo from the crazy year when we actually managed to finish this fun project?

Having lived in the beautiful Black Hills of South Dakota most of my life, I was fortunate to be able to see the 4th of July fireworks at Mount Rushmore National Memorial multiple times, even though the event took a decade long hiatus in 2009 (largely due to fire danger). So when the 2020 event was announced, I got excited to photograph the fireworks once again!

Thinking back… I could only remember photographing the fireworks once! What?!?! That can't be right… but a glance back through old files and film produced just a couple pages of Velvia 50 slide film. They were from back in 2001, taken while on a visit home during my college years.

Back then, the 4th of July fireworks display at the monument was a first come, first serve event, save for a small section at the amphitheater with reserved seating. My grandfather had thoughtfully purchased a couple of seats, and he was kind enough to give me his tickets so I could photograph the event for the first time.

The 2001 tickets did NOT, however, include a reserved parking spot! I took my boyfriend at the time and we had to walk up almost the entire hill out of Keystone, the tourist town a few miles below Mount Rushmore. It was a climb! But it was a good thing afterwards – traffic was so backed up leaving the memorial that we were walking faster than the cars were moving.

▲ The smoky & colorful 2001 fireworks display

Seriously, we passed cars on foot! The trek was well worth the experience though, and I was excited to see what I had captured.

As you can guess, 20 years ago I thought my images were amazing. Digital era photographers will never know the stress of shooting slide film… your exposure has to be spot-on, but the color you get when you do it right is sooooo pretty. I love how the old bulbs they used to light Mount Rushmore gave the rocks a green cast while the bulbs warmed up, and how it complemented the bright colors of the fireworks. Such a unique look!

But to give some perspective: out of about 72 shots from that night, I ended up with only 2-3 images I liked. I knew I had to get out there for the 2020 display and capture this momentous event with my new gear. What difference does 20 years make? Well for one thing, out of about 85 shots taken, I ended up with 55 shots that I liked. Talk about an advancement in my skills! Yeah! (It's always nice to see your hard work pay off.)

I was so happy to have more "keepers" in 2020, and not just as proof of my personal growth. Why else, you ask? Well, how about needing positive results after 10 HOURS of sweltering in 90 degree heat!

Before I dive into all the "What the f?" moments in this story, let's address the elephant in the room. The year 2020 is rife with politics, protests and a global pandemic. I do not plan to touch base on any of those topics, or my thoughts on things one way or another, during the telling of this story. This book was largely written for laughs, smiles, and inspiration, and the hot topics of 2020 are widely discussed in plenty of other places.

And yes, this story definitely has enough "What the f?" moments on it's own without the additional craziness of the year 2020!

The Return of Celebration After a 10+ year hiatus, fireworks return to Mount Rushmore National Memorial, honoring Independence Day – Black Hills of South Dakota, USA July 2020

The return of the Mount Rushmore Independence Day fireworks display was a surprise in itself, but the first time my brain went, "Wait… what???" was when they announced you'd need a ticket to attend, and those tickets would be doled out via lottery. Heck, when the event day came, they actually shut down the surrounding area, just outside the town of Keystone! You couldn't get close to Mount Rushmore at all without winning a seat. Over 25,000 people put in requests of 1-6 seats per group, resulting in over 125,000 hopefuls. Only 7,500 seats were given out.

I didn't stress about getting in to the main area, however. I'd occasionally photographed events for the local newspaper, the Rapid City Journal, and they were excited for me to shoot the event! I was counting on that press pass to get me in, parking and all.

You know the saying about not putting all your eggs in one basket? Yeah… with the president himself coming to the event, press access was limited and just three short days before the event, I found out I wouldn't be getting in.

All right, time for Plan B!

On Wednesday July 1st, two days before the event (fireworks were scheduled for Friday the 3rd), I grabbed my trusty buddy Toni and we headed for the twisty turns and tunnels of Iron Mountain Road. Other than being well known as a fun, unique drive for bikers and tourists, Iron Mountain Road has far-off views of Mount Rushmore, including famous tunnels that perfectly frame the monument if you drive from the right direction. If I could find the right spot with a composition I liked, I hoped my gear could handle the distance and capture the fireworks.

We had a heck of surprise that day when we were hiking through some trees and the loud roar of a massive engine rumbled overhead! What the….?!?! We couldn't see any planes from where we were at, but it sounded like they were flying crazy low!

We climbed to a viewpoint and the mystery was solved – the local air force pilots were practicing flyovers for Friday's event! Not only

▲ The impressive Blue Angels practicing formations, flying from behind Mount Rushmore on July 1st, two days before the event

were we amazed at the sound of the B-1s seeming to shake the air, but we got a special treat seeing the famed Blue Angels flying from behind Mount Rushmore and branching out with twists and flips in their jets. It was an unexpected and amazing experience.

With that incredible sight and the finding of the perfect shooting location atop one of the famed tunnels, Plan B was shaping out to be a great way to catch the event!

I knew that the 2020 traffic was going to be even crazier than 2001 had been, and I started to worry. I'd have to drive the back way through the hills to get to my spot on Iron Mountain Road. Since I was sure a ton of other people would have the same idea, it would be a gamble on whether or not I'd have anywhere to park. Iron Mountain Road is narrow and has no shoulder, and only offers occasional pull-offs for parking.

Thursday night I packed my gear, bringing both my D810 and the Z7 so I could do stills and video simultaneously. It's actually really difficult to watch an event that you're photographing! I knew I'd want to see the full display uninterrupted, and it would be a good test for the Z7's video capabilities.

I planned on leaving at noon. That should be plenty of time, right? I packed water, snacks, TP just in case… and thank God I found an umbrella to take! Oh yeah, I haven't clarified about the weather yet… I'd be sitting on a rocky surface, roasting in 90-DEGREE TEMPS for the entire afternoon and evening. Sunset in summer was at 9 pm.

That night there was talk all over social media about the event, and locals were speculating about taking off into the hills to find somewhere to watch the fireworks. I got nervous about my departure time and contemplated leaving earlier. That would mean close to 10 HOURS melting in the heat. But my brain didn't care! I woke up excited and was ready to go by 9am, so off I went.

As I wound my way up the back roads on the long drive to my vantage point, I knew I'd made the right call taking off early. Tons of people were already sitting at various points along the road waiting for the fireworks! Any spot where you could catch a glimpse of the memorial had tourists and locals alike looking to claim their spot (license plate Bingo, anyone?).

I was getting nervous. Was I already too late? Could I even get to my spot? I mean, I ~obviously~ picked the best view, so it had to be taken… and sure enough, I had a moment of panic when I arrived at the spot where I planned to park. A car occupied most of the pull-out. Argh! I missed my compact Fiesta, it would've fit easily… but my vehicle was still smaller than most. I eyed the spot. Should I?

I carefully maneuvered in and was surprised it fit perfectly! Encouraged by seeing only one carload of occupants on this side of the tunnel, I loaded up my gear and hoofed it up to my spot.

Aaaaaaaand it was taken.

I'd picked out a lovely flat-ish area with a clear view as my ideal shooting spot, but it also happened to be the perfect spot for the father and daughter who'd camped there all night to set up their tent. They were saving space, above and in the parking spot below, for the large group of people who would be joining them.

Now that is dedication! Though it caused me to miss out on my prime spot, I was happy to have slept the night away cozy in my bed at home. And hey, nature gives us room to adapt! The slanted spot I ended up in actually afforded me privacy throughout the day as other latecomers chose more comfortable spots elsewhere to sit. I was partially behind a ponderosa pine, but it wouldn't be in the way of either camera's shot and it only blocked my view while I slumped under the umbrella during the heat of the day. So far, so good!

All in all it was a pretty boring day filled with good company - my neighbors ended up being nice people, even though they stole my spot, ha! Though I'm normally a pretty shy and solitary person, I was grateful for their occasional visits, especially since my entertainment for the day fell through! I'd brought a book but hadn't thought to bring any way to prop up my umbrella without holding it…. so I sat allllll day holding the umbrella at just the right angle. Yes, it took both hands. Hey, I have small hands!

I did get to take a few breaks - even one to use the port-a-potty! Yep, you read that right, there was a port-a-potty! Thankfully some genius realized there'd be crowds of people hanging out in the woods away from bathrooms… and most people don't think ahead to prepare for that situation! I mean, I came prepared to pee in the woods and pack out the TP, but I was very grateful I didn't have to! Whoever thought of the port-a-potties deserves a raise. (You hear that, powers-that-be?)

Eventually the conversation turned to news (bound to happen in 2020…) and we heard about protesters blocking two of the routes to Mount Rushmore! It really was a WTF moment to be sitting in the middle of the woods knowing that the National Guard was just a few miles away dealing with a protest situation. At one point I captured a shot of a large puff of smoke coming up out of the trees. I'm pretty certain it was tear gas.

It was tense for while as various updates rolled in, but the situation was eventually as resolved as it could be. (Again, there's so

▶ My original spot may have been occupied, but I still did pretty good from my own toasty rock!

◀◀ Even far away from Mount Rushmore, people still lined the narrow roads below

▲ The president first did a flyover in Air Force One, then later landed in choppers from the nearby Ellsworth Air Force Base

145

▲ See? Hard to pick a favorite!

By this time I'd been out in the heat for hours… so perhaps it's no surprise that the rest of the day's WTF moments were not the happiest ones!

As the speech was ending, a young couple snuck up next to me and squeezed in to sit on the slanted rock.

I caught tidbits of their conversation as I worked with my cameras. They chatted away on the phone about leaving Rapid City at 7pm and just getting there at 9:15pm, and oh they have such an amazing view, blah, blah, blah. Eventually I leaned over and casually said, "So… you just got here, huh? How far away did you park?" I admit I was tired from the heat and a little cranky at this point and, knowing how full the parking spots had been for hours, was expecting a little vindication with news of a long trek for the intruders.

"Oh, we're just on the other side of the tunnel. We rode a motorcycle."

So much for that. It's a good thing it was dark at this point, as I'm fairly certain I had an involuntary scowl on my face while I thought about sitting in the sweltering heat all day! Sheesh, I would have loved to have spent the day home in the AC with my hubby and pups before casually popping out to get a prime view and…

BOOM! The show started and I forgot all my troubles.

I will never tire of seeing brilliant, colorful fireworks above Mount Rushmore. And these were different, a new high-tech variety that produced less smoke and was less likely to spark a forest fire. The festive celebrations remind me of so many wonderful memories with my family, especially my grandfather who was such a big influence on my life. He would've loved the show.

All good things must come to an end of course, and apparently I was doomed to a return of the crankiness after the euphoria of watching the fireworks faded. I was tired and achy from baking in the heat all day, and now I had to try to make my way home… just like the bazillion other people out there. My original plan was to go back the way I'd come, which would immediately take me through a series of narrow one-way tunnels.

much more that happened elsewhere that day, but I'm only sharing my observations from afar.)

The show would go on! A bit more of a show than expected, actually. We came for fireworks and got a procession. Air Force One did a flyover before landing at Ellsworth Air Force Base 30 miles away, and social media was abuzz with news that the president had landed. Not long after, numerous helicopters and osprey landed at the monument and the military aerial planes put on their show. Of course the sun had now set right behind the monument, ugh! Everyone knows it's tough to shoot directly into the sun, but I was able to capture a few unique images.

And I was here for the fireworks anyway!

The road below was filled with onlookers now, and everyone crowded around their phones for the president's speech. South Dakota is a small electoral state, so a presidential visit - at Mount Rushmore, no less! - is a pretty big deal, regardless of what side of the fence you prefer. I snuck a peak at my neighbor's phone but quickly stepped away from the crowd. Ha, "social distancing" is an easy concept for us shy folk!

Bad idea. I repeat, BAD idea.

Normally when there's light or just normal traffic on Iron Mountain Road, vehicles take turns going each way through the one-way tunnels. A line of two or three cars might go through together as cars coming the other direction wait their turn. But all common decency went out the window that night.

Getting through that first tunnel was an utter nightmare. I spent a good 20 minutes or more honking like a lunatic, waving my arms and yelling to try and get the flow of cars from the other direction to pause and let our side through. No one cared. I won't lie – I'm rather embarrassed by my crazy behavior, but it had been a looooong HOT day. What can I say? I snapped!

I finally had a brief chance as the caravan of traffic seemed to end and I entered the tunnel… as did the a-hole at the other end. Even though he saw me in the tunnel, he kept on coming. Who'd expect to have an old west style stand-off in your car?!? Being the smaller vehicle I was forced to back up out of the tunnel. I might have yelled at them as they drove by. Just a little. Sigh… I repeat, I'm not proud of my behavior, but it really irks me when people are so inconsiderate.

After I finally made it through the tunnel, it dawned on me that I'd have to go through TWO MORE tunnels. Since I honestly NEVER get that irate when driving, I decided I couldn't handle it and turned around. I'd rather brave the heavy traffic through Keystone. And yes, I was nice and took turns on the way back through!

One headache and two hours later, I finally collapsed in bed at the end of my 15-hour excursion.

I'm always excited to look at my images when I get home from a shoot. I'm like a little kid and can't wait, often downloading and processing right away, so I practically ran to the computer the next morning to finally see what I got! I expected a repeat of 2001 with only a couple of good images, and thought the image quality might be low with me having been so far away… but I found crisp shots all the way through! I could hardly pick my favorites and couldn't wait to share them!

I was short on time though, as this was the official 4th of July and we had a family barbecue to get to. I quickly processed several shots, submitted a few to the local paper, then scrambled to post them on Facebook, only having enough time to type "Ta da!" for the post.

Two hours later, I was stunned to have the most likes and shares that I'd ever had for my images. What the… nobody shares my stuff! How did I suddenly get over 70,000 reactions and 1,200 shares?!?!

▲ The new high-tech fireworks were far less smoky!

Best WTF ever!!!

I was completely unprepared. People wanted to buy prints and I didn't even have an online store! (When Covid hit, I took my online store down for much needed maintenance.) I scrambled to get the images online for purchase that night, and I spent the next day reaching out to everyone who had inquired about them. It was the most wonderful and exhausting day of correspondence ever!

In the end my post was seen by over half a million people (!!!) and shared over 4,000 times.

Not only did my long day in the heat result in my most popular images to date, but they saved my year financially as well. Most of my print sales usually occur at various festivals and art shows throughout the year, but the pandemic cancelled all of them in 2020. By the end of the summer, this single event wiped out all of that lost income and kept me afloat.

If you are reading this story and you bought a print: from the bottom of my heart, THANK YOU. I cannot thank you enough for the love and support you showed me and my dream.

And if you're a (I hope) happy owner of this book, thank you too! Never in my wildest dreams did I think I would actually get to make a book of my photos AND my stories, then have people BUY it and READ it! So cool! This project was definitely a blast.

Thank you all for going on this journey with me. I hope you've laughed and smiled. I hope you love my images, and I hope you've come away vowing to never again say "someday." What are your dreams? What have you been putting off until "someday?" Don't wait. Start making a plan NOW and just go for it!

Otherwise you'll never know what kind of wonderful adventures may be waiting for you.

> "Thank you... for going on this journey with me."

the end

JUST KIDDING!

We've come to the end of the stories, but there's more. Read on for a collection of my favorite photography tips!

TOP 5

Are you ready for my
Top 5/Top 5?
Read on for my five favorite tips in five photographic categories!

Portraits by Johnny Sundby

share time

with Erica Lane Harvey

M. Photog. Cr., CPP | Erica Lane Photography, LLC

Here's something that may surprise those who know me: I get super nervous talking to people, especially to crowds! I even had to have my best friend Toni step out of the room when she was helping me film sound bytes for our Kickstarter video to promote this book.

But it's a different story at art shows and events! I love setting up my booth and chatting with people as they stop by to check out my images. I still start out a bit nervous, but once I get caught up in chatting about the joy of doing what I do, the nerves just go away.

Every once in a while a fellow photographer will stop by, and then I can really get going as we talk about what camera was used, which lens, what time of day, what settings, etc. So of course, this is when I start sharing my favorite photography tips!

This book started as a coffee table book, but then I decided to add all the stories that I'd usually share at various art shows and events. After that, it was just a natural fit to share all the other stuff I chat about at shows!

The shooting and editing tips only touch the surface of what I do to capture my images, as anyone who's attended one of my workshops or classes will know. But they cover some of the best tools in my arsenal. And being a nature lover, it follows that wildlife hot spots and gorgeous locations make the list as well.

I hope you enjoy my Top 5 lists!

NIKON D810

1. **Think Tank Filter Nest Mini** with:
   » Hoya 77mm UV Filter
   » Hoya 77mm Circular Polarizer
   » Hoya 77mm ND8 Filter (3-stop Neutral Density)
2. **Hoodman HoodEYE**
3. **Silica Packets**
4. **Extra EN-EL15 Batteries**
5. **Tool Kit** *(mini screwdriver & such)*
6. **Microfiber Lens Cloths**
7. **Headlamp with White & Red Lights**
8. **Ulanzi ST-03 iPhone Tripod Attachment**
   » Dovetail Quick Release System
9. **Nikon MC-30A Remote Trigger Release**

1. **Wimberley, The Sidekick SK-100**
   » Dovetail Quick Release System
2. **Really Right Stuff (RSS) Ball Head, BH-55**
   » Dovetail Quick Release System
3. **RSS Carbon-Fiber Tripod, TVC-24**
4. **RSS Carbon-Fiber Tripod, TFC-14**
5. **RSS Ball Head, BH-30**
   » Dovetail Quick Release System
6. **Bear Spray** *(whichever brand is available)*
7. **AF-S Nikkor 300mm f/2.8G ED VR II**
8. **Detachable Neck Strap** *(no longer available)*
9. **Ruggard SD & CF Card Cases**
10. **LEE SW150 Field Pouch** with:
    » LEE SW150 Neutral Density Grad Set – Soft
    » LEE SW150 Big Stopper
    » LEE SW150 Circular Polarizer
11. **Nikon DSLR D810 36 MP**
    » RRS Nikon D810 L-Plate, BD810-L
12. **AF-S Nikkor 14-24mm f/2.8G ED**
13. **AF-S Zoom-Nikkor 17-35mm f/2.8D IF-ED**
14. **SW150 Mark II Filter Holder & Nikon 14-24mm Lens Adapter**
15. **NIkkor AF-S Teleconverter TC-20E III 2x**
16. **NIkkor AF-S Teleconverter TC-14E II 1.4x**
17. **Storm Jacket – Large**
18. **Storm Jacket – Medium** *Tip: I colored in the "M" and the logo to tell these bags apart.*
19. **AF-S Nikkor 70-200mm f/2.8G ED VR II**
20. **AF-S Micro-Nikkor 105mm f/2.8G IF-ED VR**
21. **AF-S Zoom-NIkkor 28-70mm f/2.8D**
22. **SW150 Screw-in Lens Adapter 77mm**
23. **Bandana** *(always handy)*
24. **Bug Net** *(it really helps when needed)*
25. **Epi-Pen** *(I've got bee allergies)*
26. **Wool Buff**
27. **Clip** *(to hang bag on tripod)*
28. **Bubble Level for Flash Shoe**
29. **NOVOFLEX MagicBalance**
30. **NOVOFLEX Panorama VR-System II** *(L-Bracket not shown, RSS L-Plate in use)*

MAIN SET-UP

23 lbs

Weight also includes:
MindShift BackLight 26L

152

THE CAMERAS
NIKON Z7

HIKING SET-UP
17.2 lbs

Weight also includes: MindShift BackLight 18L, RSS Small Tripod & Nikkor 70-200 f/2.8

1. **ThinkTank Filter Nest Mini with:**
   - K&F 82mm Circular Polarizer
   - Tamron 72mm Circular Polarizer
   - 72-77mm Step-Up Ring
   - Cokin 77MM Adaptor
2. **Nikon Mirrorless Z7 45MP**
   - RRS Nikon Z7 Ultralight L-Plate, BZ7-L
3. Peak Design Leash Neck Strap
4. **ThinkTank MindShift Filter Hive**
   - Cokin Z-Pro Neutral Density Graduated Filter Set
5. Microfiber Lens Cloth
6. Nikkor Z 14-30mm f/4 S
7. Nikkor Z 24-70mm f/4 S
8. Nikon Mount Adapter FTZ
9. Wool Buff
10. Cokin Z-Pro Filter Holder with 82mm Adapter Ring
11. Cokin 77mm Adapter Ring
12. Peak Design Extra Parts and Tool
13. ThinkTank Pixel Pocket XQD Card Holder
14. Nikon MC-DC2 Remote Release Cord

If the Gear Fits...

Ever since I discovered long ago that Nikon is the perfect fit for my little hands, I've been building up my photography arsenal!

Outside of my camera and lenses, there are quite a few pieces of equipment I find essential to my success when creating images.

Some of these items may be considered obsolete, but I enjoy the challenge of getting my image correct with the data I need in ONE shot, in-camera. That way, minimal editing is needed when working with the RAW file.

That's a bonus for me!

Top 5/Top 5 Photography Tips:

- Quality Gear
- Shooting Tips
- Digital Editing
- Wildlife Spots
- Fav Locations

153

TOP 5

QUALITY GEAR

> " ...as close as you can get to perfect... "

◀ It has taken me quite a bit of time and investment to find the perfect gear!

The right bags, tripods, filters and other accessories make photography adventures even more enjoyable. Never settle for sub-par!

◀ I use the Tenba LL-400 bag (not mentioned in the tips) for my biggest lens, the Nikkor 300 f/2.8. I bought the large size bag so I can leave the lens hood attached at all times. Works great!

Erica's Top 5: Quality Gear

1. MindShift from Think Tank® Photo

When it comes to photography bags, functionality is key. Every photographer needs a bag that balances gear with shooting habits, and we're all different. Because most of us haul around a heavy load of equipment, the bag can literally make or break you… especially your back!

Photographers are always on the lookout for the perfect bag, and after 25 years of using so-so bags, I finally discovered **MindShift from Think Tank Photo®**. Their bags seem to be built just for me, and I discovered firsthand that **their customer service is exceptional!** I put my first MindShift bag through the wringer on my travels, and a bit of the stitching had started to wear out. While at a photography conference, I mentioned this to a Think Tank Photo® sales rep and he immediately helped me get approved for a replacement bag! Once home I said a teary farewell to my old bag before shipping it off, and quickly received my new bag. Slick!

I'm not alone in my opinion - many of my photographer friends also tout these as "the perfect bags." The model I use is the **MindShift BackLight 26L (also available in 18L, 36L and 45L)**. I use it to haul my main set-up, and it allows me to pack my D810 gear with easy access to all the extras. It has **handy straps for adjusting to a comfortable fit**. And speaking of fit – it slides nicely under the seat of a plane for easy carry-on!

Don't be misled by my needing to get the first bag replaced – with the weight of all the gear I haul around, it's amazing the straps hadn't just given out and popped off! **These bags from Think Tank Photo® are extremely well made** and have held up impressively.

I am so in love with these bags that I've since bought the 18L size for my Z7 hiking kit. They are as close as you can get to perfect, in my opinion. All that's missing are straps on the bottom for me to attach my jacket… hopefully they'll add that on the next models, but for now, I've just sewn on my own straps!

Erica's Top 5: Quality Gear

2 Really Right Stuff® Tripods

Every new photographer who just spent money on a camera and lens tends to make the choice to save money on accessories, especially when it comes to the tripod. A word of advice: **DON'T GO CHEAP!**

I wish I'd taken that advice six tripods ago. SIX tripods you ask? Oh yes. In college I went with "sturdy" options in my low budget range, and learned the hard way they were just a ridiculous lunk of weight to haul around. I tried light weight options next (still low budget), and shouldn't have been surprised when I came home with soft images. Ugh!

The saying "you get what you pay for" is definitely accurate for tripods. A good friend of mine finally introduced me to the Really Right Stuff® brand, and I haven't looked back! I have two tripods that I've invested in, and they're such top notch quality that they'll be with me for life.

The truly crazy part is that the RRS tripods are so light, even the larger one is lighter than any of the cheap tripods I'd purchased before! And they function beautifully. I love how quickly they expand and collapse, how easily they come apart for cleaning, and – BONUS – they're made in the USA!

I'll be honest – each tripod was very pricey, especially with the ball head and other attachments I've added. However, the cost ended up being equal to what I'd spent while trying out the "in my budget" tripods, so I may as well have bitten the bullet and bought a quality RRS set-up at the start! I'd have saved myself multiple headaches.

I should also mention the RRS tripods feature a spring-loaded dovetail quick-release system that makes it easy to flip from vertical to horizontal on an L-plate, all the while keeping my camera centered over the tripod to maintain the stability needed for long exposures. Truly, the design and functionality just make sense, and these quality tripods are worth the investment.

I've been using these tripods for over four years now, and even though they're full of scratches and dings, they still work great. However many travels and adventures I take them on, they keep on getting the job done!

Graduated filters add beautiful balance to the exposure at the time of shooting. In instances like the image to the right, I'll rotate the filter on the front of the camera to follow the horizon line. I love the result! The gradation in the sky ends up drawing the eye into the image.

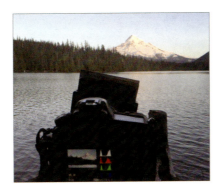

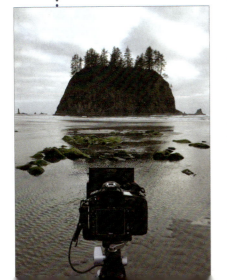

Erica's Top 5: Quality Gear

3 Graduated Filters

This is actually a bit of a heated topic. With the capabilities of high quality sensors and computer editing, there are discussions in the photography world about whether filters are a tool that's even needed when you're out shooting.

My personal answer is YES! But why bother with actual filters when you can just edit in a filter effect later, you ask? I feel **the more data you can capture in the RAW file when you're shooting, the better quality the image will be in the end**. If the exposure data isn't balanced in the first place, you won't be able to pull out any detail in your highlights and shadows during digital processing.

Graduated filters allow you to balance out the bright and dark areas as the light enters your lens. And quality is important – don't go cheap on graduated filters or you might get color shifts and degradation in your image. These filters are mainly used at sunrise and sunset to darken the bright sky and allow you to expose properly for detail in the shadow areas. If you want to see some examples where I've used graduated filters, **check out the stories on pages 46, 60, 76, 82, and 136.**

Using these filters lets me create the popular HDR look with detailed exposures throughout the photo, all without manually combining the images in Photoshop® or masking in the sky. I love anything that cuts down on my editing time, so the extra effort when I'm out shooting is absolutely worth the beautiful results!

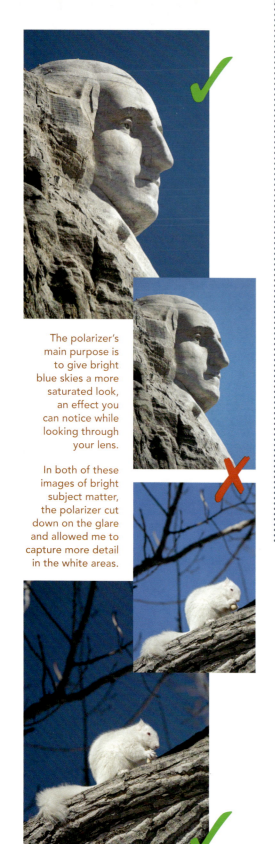

The polarizer's main purpose is to give bright blue skies a more saturated look, an effect you can notice while looking through your lens.

In both of these images of bright subject matter, the polarizer cut down on the glare and allowed me to capture more detail in the white areas.

Erica's Top 5: Quality Gear
4 Circular Polarizer

Another filter that tends to get overlooked in lieu of using digital filter effects is the **circular polarizer**. Quite a few photographers actually use this filter more as a lens protector, since it screws securely onto the front of your lens. Alas, that is NOT it's main purpose.

Many computer programs offer a "polarizing filter," but **no computer can mimic the full effect of the real thing**. So what does the polarizer do? I'm glad you asked! If you have a polarizing filter, you'll notice that it can be rotated on the front of your lens without unscrewing. **When rotated, you'll notice this piece of glass will darken the sky and reduce glare.**

I've used polarizers enough to know a computer filter is no substitute for the real thing. The filters are cheap and easy to leave on your camera (yes, it's cheaper to scratch the filter than your lens, so it IS a good lens protector as well), so you may as well make good use of it! Just note that the tint in a polarizer blocks some light, so it's best to take it off for sunrises and sunsets.

I'll wait here while you go order one and stick it on the end of your lens. Got it? Awesome! Now just **make sure you pay attention to HOW it's rotated, especially if you flip your camera.** Everyone forgets that at some point, ha! ("Why is my vertical shot darker than my horiz… oh, yeah, polarizer.")

Here's a polarizer pro tip: don't use it with too wide of a lens! It can't cover the entire scene and you'll end up with unnatural gradation from light to dark. The image below shot at 19mm shows this unwanted effect.

A carabiner is easy to attach and detach, but a bandana works in a pinch! I keep both attached to the handle of my bag.

Erica's Top 5: Quality Gear

5 Carabiner Clip

This last tip gives a nod to a **simple yet effective tool that I've begun to use more as of late: a simple clip**. In short, a good clip helps me stabilize my tripod by hanging the weight of my bag under the tripod.

When shooting with a slow or long exposure, stabilizing your tripod is a must, and clipping weight to the tripod makes a difference. A number of things can shake even the sturdiest of tripods, from a gust of wind to the footsteps of passersby **(see story on page 50)**. I've missed a few shots for these reasons!

The first time I hung my bag under the tripod was just to keep it out of the mud, ha! All I had to attach it at the time was my bandana, but hey, it worked. Heck, the extra weight worked so well that I invested in a **sturdy S-Biner** (a 2-sided carabiner clip) so I could quickly attach my bag once I'm set up.

I've taken to always attaching my bag to the tripod when shooting my sunset and low-light work. The extra 15 pounds is a great stabilizer… especially at night when you tend to bump into things! That's when it gives you a little peace of mind as well, like when I photographed the 2020 Mt. Rushmore fireworks **(see bonus story on page 142)**. Not only did the weight of my bag add stabilization for my six and eight second exposures, but it added security against me accidentally knocking my gear off the cliff!

SHOOTING TIPS

Erica's Top 5: Shooting Tips

1 Clean & Simple

If it's not part of the story, just get rid of it! Everything you can see in the viewfinder contributes to the composition and story your image tells, so I try to look at every scene with the intent of drawing focus to my subject and highlighting my story.

Before I take my picture, I'm in the habit of scanning two particular areas:

> **The Edges** - are there distracting elements on the edges of the frame you can remove by zooming or changing position?

> **Behind the Subject** - is there anything odd or distracting behind your subject that's drawing attention away from the subject?

By keeping your image clean and simple, you're making it easier for the viewer to capture the feeling and find your story. Once you've mastered the clean and simple images, you'll be better prepared to compose more complicated scenes and still be able to tell your story.

These images were shot at Sylvan Lake in Custer State Park, South Dakota, and cleaning up the composition vastly improved the final shot on the bottom.

In the top image, the foreground ended up distracting from the beautiful lake and unique rock structures that form the backdrop of what should be a stunning scene. At that angle I couldn't avoid the foreground distracting from my desired subject: the unique little rocky islands.

By removing the foreground and leaving more space around the edges of the elements, I captured a much cleaner image that brings your focus to the interesting rocks and gives you a clear view of the reflection in the water.

DEPTH OF FIELD

f/2.8
f/4
f/5.6
f/8
f/11
f/16

Aperture: f/13
The higher f-stop keeps more of the subject in focus, but getting close with the camera lens still throws the background out of focus.

Aperture: f/3.5
A fast lens can let you open up the aperture very wide, creating much shallower depth of field and the blurred effect known as bokeh.

DIGITAL EDITING

Erica's Top 5: Editing Tips

1 The Power of RAW

This first editing tip is the most important and happens before you even get to your computer. **You MUST shoot in RAW to get the most out of your editing process.** A RAW image gives you the best possible chance to edit and retouch your file, especially when working with natural light. The goal is to capture data without blowing out shadows and highlights, especially with sunrises and sunsets where you often have to push your exposure to the limit.

With digital cameras, you get instant gratification by viewing your images immediately on your camera's screen. However, it's important to note that this is **NOT an accurate way to gauge exposure** – the image you see on the **camera screen is just an interpretation** of the captured data. Therefore, **the best way to gauge data is by looking at the histogram.**

With RAW, the goal is to **capture as much data as possible,** and the **histogram** is the tool that shows you an accurate representation of how much **light, dark and mid-tone data** you captured in an image.

Typical histograms like the Adobe® Lightroom® samples on this page show:

- Blacks/shadow values on the left
- White/highlight values on the right
- Mid-tones in between
- Overall exposure is shown in grey
- RGB values are shown in their respective colors
- Anything going off the left or right means loss of detail

Histogram measurements will look a bit like a mountain range. **The ideal exposure creates a nice "bell" shaped curve on your histogram**, like the final image on the opposite page. In normal light, you can use your camera's histogram to help you expose for a centered bell curve.

Balancing the difference between shadows and highlights can be tough, especial at sunrise and sunset, the ideal shooting times. In extreme light such as these times, it's perfectly acceptable – even ideal – for that curve to be more

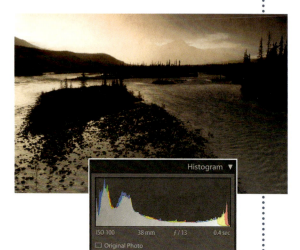

STEP 1: RAW Data
This histogram has heavy information on the left side of the diagram, which means dark shadows in the image. There is still enough data within the histogram to indicate the shadows are not completely blocked up, and we have detail that can be worked with in digital processing.

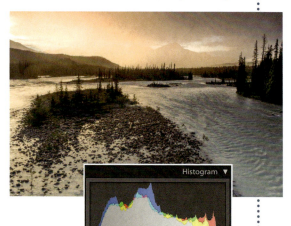

STEP 2: Adobe® Lightroom® Adjustments
By making adjustments in Lightroom® we've now brought back more of the midtone range. The histogram now tells us we have data in all the areas. The image looks flat here, but will come to life with further processing!

FINAL STEP 3: *Photoshop® and Nik® Processing* Programs like Adobe® Photoshop® and DxO® Nik® allow us to push histogram values to a more ideal shape, curved like a bell. I originally thought this image was a bust, but look at the detail I was able to recover!

To Avoid: Clipping ▼
The "develop" mode histogram in Adobe® Lightroom® will show a highlighted triangle at the top left or right corner if you're losing detail. This is called clipping because valuable information has been cut, causing image degradation.

A white triangle on the left means your shadows are losing detail, and the same on the right means loss of highlight detail. If the triangles are red, green or blue, it's telling you that you've lost highlight or shadow detail for that specific color range.

to the left (for dark scenes, like the Step 1 histogram) or to the right (when the scene is bright). The ultimate goal is to not have any blown-out highlights or blocked-up blacks, indicated in the histogram when the values go off the sides of the diagram.

Keeping everything inside the histogram means you have detail in ALL areas of your image. You can recover things a little bit, like I did for the shadows in this image. In landscape photography, it can be acceptable to have slight loss of detail in the highlights and shadows since we're often dealing with extreme light.

Here's a pro tip: I suggest trying to get the peak of the bell to fall a bit right of where they would fall for a "normal" exposure – in essence, **go for slightly brighter shadow values when shooting.** When you lighten dark areas during the digital editing step, your shadows will end up looking grainy or muddy if you push them too far. I compensate by exposing my shadows a touch lighter than normal. (I didn't do this for the sample image on this page because I would have blown out the highlights.)

You can even take it farther! If you can't get the perfect exposure in one shot, the histogram helps you shoot and analyze multiple shots of a scene so you can expose for the different areas and blend the images together later in Adobe® Photoshop® – it's best to use a tripod for this method so the images match up easily.

In short, **the histogram is a valuable tool, so take advantage of it!**

Adobe product screenshot(s) throughout the "Top 5 Editing Tips" section are reprinted with permission from Adobe.
Adobe® Lightroom® and Adobe® Photoshop® are either registered trademarks or trademarks of Adobe in the United States and/or other countries.

Erica's Top 5: Editing Tips

2 Adobe® Lightroom®

Adobe® Lightroom® is the first program I use for digital editing. This amazing program mimics old-school darkroom processing, with the addition of digital editing tools to accommodate advancing technology.

There are a few automated tools I use when opening a file:

1) I open the **"Lens Corrections"** *tab and check* **"Remove Chromatic Aberrations"** *– see top left graphic. This will remove the magenta and green lines you often see in images shot with older lenses.*

2) I might also click **"Enable Profile Corrections,"** *which will fix lens distortion based on the specific lens you used to create the image.*

From here I play with the **sliders for highlight and shadow detail, texture, clarity, vibrance, and color temperature (see the graphic to the left)** before I open in Photoshop® to remove the inevitable dust spots. (Lightroom® has its own spot remover, but I prefer the technique I go over in my next tip.)

When you first open a RAW file it looks muddy and flat, and it is our job as an artist to showcase the image at its best. For me this means **recreating** what I saw; for others it might mean **enhancing** the image beyond what they saw. Neither is wrong, just be sure you accurately represent yourself to the viewer, especially if you add something such as a fake sky or other elements. My personal goal with most of my landscape work is conservation, so I want to make sure what I show is a real moment, not a fabricated scene. (Lately I've delved into digital painting, and I go more artistic and surreal with the images.)

The best part about Lightroom® is you are doing **non-destructive editing**. So if you had an off night editing and thought "What the F was I thinking?" – well, the next day all you have to do is hit the reset button to start over! Plus, you can even copy and paste your adjustments from one image and apply them to another or a group of images – also called syncing. What a time saver!

You can use these tools on just about any file format in Lightroom®, but they're best done on a RAW file that has the most image data to work with.

Can you believe this is the same image? The RAW file to the left may appear too dark, but the histograms on the camera when shooting told me I was capturing all kinds of beautiful detail that I could later pull out in Adobe® Lightroom®.

Erica's Top 5: Editing Tips
3 Adobe® Photoshop®

Once I'm done with my usual Lightroom® adjustments, I move on to **Adobe® Photoshop®** for detailing. At first this program is overwhelming for most – it has SO many amazing tools that can be used in various ways – but for the purposes of landscape and wildlife, **we'll focus on the ability to clean up dust!** There are several "clean-up" tools that all accomplish the same task of fixing problem spots, but my favorites are:

- the amazing Spot Healing Brush tool (plus the Patch tool in the sub-menu)
- the classic Clone Stamp tool (hey, if it ain't broke, don't fix it!)

In the beginning it was just me, **the Clone Stamp tool, and lots of clicking**. It allows you to select a spot in your photo and then copy it to another spot. It's great for removing dust and other small unwanted spots in your image... but it's best for small, easy fixes.

I was so happy when I discovered the **Spot Healing Brush,** or "band-aid" tool as it's commonly called. It's like the Clone Stamp but with artificial intelligence built in! Instead of selecting a spot to clone, you just **brush over the ugly spot and TA-DA, it's gone!** Well... most of the time, ha! Nothing is perfect and you sometimes have to take a mulligan, or just go back and forth between multiple tools to get it juuuuuust right. Keyboard shortcuts help!

These tools are great for removing blemishes such as the **common spots that are a result of dust building up on your camera sensor.** It's inevitable that dust will invade if you change lenses, as you can see in my sample images above! FYI: when your images look this dirty, send your camera in for professional cleaning - I did after this image and it was vastly improved! I also target weird grass or dirty fur in my nature shots, but the tools are great for skin blemishes in portraiture as well. The "patch" tool is another one to practice with - it comes in handy when having to fix large areas.

Like pretty much anything in the Photoshop® toolbox, **these tools take practice to learn their limits, and time to learn how to work with their imperfections.** Many of you, I hope, already use these tools... if not, I highly recommend giving them a try!

Photoshop® can do SO much more, of course, but I wanted to highlight my two favorite tools. And if I tried to get into anything else, this would be a 500-page book! It's an amazing program. If you're curious about a tool, just play with it! You can always visit the Adobe® forum or search online for helpful videos to get you started. Have fun!

Erica's Top 5: Editing Tips

4 The Evolution of Nik®

This tip happens to have a What the f? moment! You see, I have been a fan of the **Nik® software collection** since first purchasing it back in 2014. What I didn't realize is that Google actually owned the company. The rumor is they were after the programmers when they bought the company in 2012, so they didn't touch the software at first.

In 2016, Google decided to give the software away for free. I repeat, for FREE, after I'd PAID for it. What the... seriously? Now everyone suddenly had easy access to what I'd always felt was my "super secret software." Bah! Google then eventually updated the software, so I had to ditch my purchased product and download their versions. Oh well, I was OK as long as they kept the software current! But then... in 2017 a company named DxO® bought it, and to keep myself up-to-date I had to buy it all over AGAIN!!!

I mostly laugh now at the evolution of this program because whatever I need to do to keep it current, IT'S WORTH IT. **This software is amazing!** Heck, there was even a period of panic before the DxO® purchase when it seemed Google might not keep the software going. I was worried, and I tell ya, I don't normally get upset over software, of all things. I wasn't alone in this – the photographic community as a whole was beyond elated that DxO® decided to take it on and keep it current.

Now, many of the things the software does can be done with other programs, but **Nik® can do it faster and better** in my opinion, especially the **Color Efex Pro App**. My favorite filters include: color contrast range, darken/lighten center, detail extractor, pro contrast, and dynamic skin softener (for portraits). **I find that this program gives my images a clean and polished look that I can't achieve on my own**. I also think nothing can top the **Silver Efex Pro App,** a stellar black and white conversion tool. These are my two favorites from the multiple apps included! Just trust me that this software is worth the investment.

There is a learning curve to using the program, of course. Remember that **masking is your friend** (use the plus and minus options). And **don't just click a filter** - select the double-box icon to see the options, it will apply much better. Like all software it's never easy on your first ride; it takes **practice, patience and time** to learn and see what works best for you and your system.

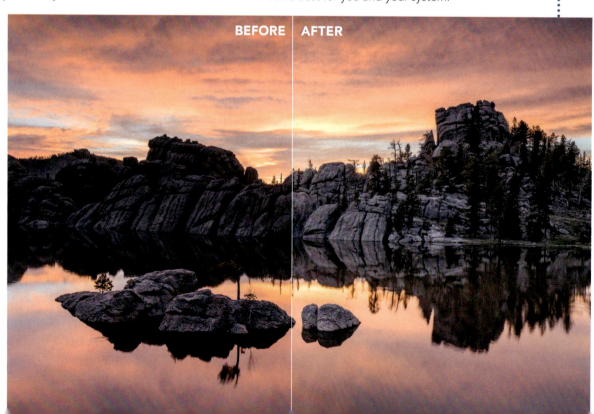

This image shows the difference before and after editing with Nik® software.

The left side shows regular digital editing, which can only take you so far. On the right, Nik® takes it the extra mile.

Notice the difference in the shadows and highlights... the fine details in the sky, water and rocks are much more evident!

Editing with Nik® can really give your image that final "POP" to make it extraordinary.

JPG 8 Compression: 4.2 MB   RAW Lossless Compression: 28.1 MB   TIFF: 128 MB   Nikon D610: 5652 x 3773 Pixels

Erica's Top 5: Editing Tips

5 The Right Format

This last "editing" tip has more to do with **saving your images for future use**. I recommend preserving your original shots in RAW format at the very least, but there's a safer way to save those files where they won't go obsolete.

In Lightroom® you may notice that it gives you the option to **import and export as a DNG file** (digital negative). It's not a format you usually hear about, so it's easy to ignore. **The purpose of a DNG is simply to preserve a generic RAW file in a universally compatible format.** Each camera made has it's own unique RAW file format and Adobe® had to make a plug-in just to work with all of them, whether new or old. It's also worth noting that RAW and DNG file sizes seem small when compared to TIFF format because the data is compressed for retrieval, referred to as "lossless compression."

There may come a time in the future that Adobe® won't support my older Nikon D2x files, so **by importing the file as a DNG, I'm making sure I can always open them in Adobe®** – they have stated they will always include the capability to open such files (or so I heard from a friend who talked with an Adobe® designer about this topic).

File format is another decision you have to make when saving out your **final processed images**. Back in 2006, I used to save as JPEG due to space issues (storage devices were pricier then). **JPEG files are not meant to preserve data**, they are meant to remove data to make the file size friendlier for online use. That data can't be retrieved, and more data is tossed each time you save a JPEG. I have tried working with some of my old JPEGs, and I eventually start to see nasty pixelation and banding. Ugh! I now only use JPEG for copies, such as when sending a converted file to a vendor or client.

I've learned it's much better to save as a TIFF or PSD, since they're non-compressed files, plus both of these files can save my layers if I have any. It takes up more space, but thankfully digital storage is more affordable now. I've already filled my eight terabyte hard drive, ha! I should have listened to the salesman and bought the 12 TB drive…

Speaking of back-ups, I'll repeat what another friend has intoned many times: **ALWAYS have three copies of your files: the original, the primary back-up, and the off-site back-up.** You never know when your house might catch on fire, or someone might accidentally knock a hard drive off your desk. I have yet to lose a drive, but I have friends who have lost hours and hours of irreplaceable work. I'd rather avoid that!

Speaking of which, I have been meaning to buy that third drive, I gotta run! **Thanks for sticking with me through the "techy" part of the tips section! Locations and wildlife are next.** I know some of my gear, shooting and editing tips are pretty basic, and some might be confusing at the get-go, but the best part about photography is there is always something to learn, and with time and practice you can make your images better and better!

TOP 5 WILDLIFE SPOTS

Erica's Top 5: Wildlife Hotspots

1 Badlands
National Park in South Dakota

Here's the crazy things about the Badlands: this wildlife hotspot was initially not even on my radar, even though I lived just a short one-hour drive away from the unique national park. Heck, I'd been to Yellowstone – over NINE hours away – before I'd been to the Badlands!

Finally in the past few years, I've begun to develop a strong connection with the little-known park. (The Badlands did have a moment of fantastic infamy in 2018, however, when it went against the presidential mandate to not mention climate change and was called the Bad-ass-lands for a while!)

The Badlands are rugged and harsh, but the park has many splendid moments of unique beauty, especially in spring when you can catch sight of all kinds of **baby animals**! From **prairie dogs** and **burrowing owls** to **bison** and **bighorn sheep**, this small but bountiful park never disappoints.

Burrowing owls are one of the unexpected treasures in Badlands National Park. Heck, I didn't even know about them until recently! (See "They have what now?!?!" on page 92.)

Much of South Dakota is ranch land, so this unfarmable park – made up of layers of sediment – provides homes to an abundance of native creatures that need room to roam. I don't think I've ever heard of someone going through the Badlands and NOT seeing wildlife!

During the hot months it's best to visit early or late in the day to avoid sweltering heat on terrain that can feel like the Sahara. Meanwhile, winter can provide great viewing all day long, but visitors should be prepared for freezing temps and icy conditions.

Sage Creek (on the west end of the park) is an area where many animals can easily be spotted. But as I mentioned, you're likely to find wildlife in almost every corner of the Badlands.

And the best part? It's not too terribly expensive to stay in the area, especially in comparison to other park areas on this list. Plus it's right next to another wildlife playground and photographer's paradise, the **Black Hills**! And I should know – I've called them home for over 35 years.

Prairie Dogs are so fun to catch sight of in the Badlands! Their "towns" are noticeable by mounds popping up from the otherwise flat, grassy areas, and their cute, inquisitive heads are easy to spot, sticking up much like meerkats.

Bighorn sheep are just a natural fit in the Badlands. The terrain is practically made for their grippy hooves, and it's a delight to watch them walk up a steep incline like it's no big deal.

Two areas are widely known for their buffalo inhabitants, and South Dakota's Black Hills and Badlands area is one of them. The other is, of course, Yellowstone, which is my next wildlife hotspot.

The bison love to roam the Badlands terrain, and their area in the park was recently expanded, bringing them closer to popular areas. The image to the left is from before, when they roamed a bit further away!

Though these fluffy beasts seem tame, they are still wild animals. Please only get close to the fluffy boulders with the use of a telephoto lens (or you might lose your pants)!

Big furry bison, frosted in ice and dusted in snow, are some of Yellowstone's most amazing winter treasures.

Erica's Top 5: Wildlife Hotspots

2 Yellowstone
National Park in Wyoming

Yellowstone is a **wildlife mecca**, especially if you take advantage of the early morning and late evening hours in spring and summer. However, the numerous visitors can make the wildlife scarce.

I personally feel if you're willing to brave the elements in winter, you will not be disappointed. The stark, white, snow-covered fields makes it easy to spot **elk** and **bison**, and fresh snow makes for clean compositions. Plus, who doesn't want to see a **fox** or **coyote** dive into the snow after mice? It's quite a site to behold!

For a first time winter visit, I suggest going with a group and letting the park do the planning. Yellowstone can be pricey and difficult to visit in winter, especially since the interior roads of the park are closed and facilities are only accessible by snow coach or snowmobile. Plan early! It's great if you find a photo group, but regular tour groups are also going to be searching for wildlife – they just don't spend more than 20 minutes with a sighted animal.

For me, the best part of winter in Yellowstone is the peace and quiet. Without the summer crowds, you are treated to an experience that harkens back to the park's early days… except you get electricity and a hot shower!

As long as you're prepared for the elements, the pricey winter tours are well worth the cost. But for a less costly winter experience, you can always stay in Gardiner, Montana and tour the open Lamar Valley area **(see Fav Locations, page 184)**. Just keep an eye out – winter tourists hauling snowmobiles use this highway to get to Cooke City, Montana, and it can be scary when those big rigs fly by!

Elk, coyotes and foxes, oh my! And swans? Neat…

An abundance of wildlife roams free in Yellowstone National Park, including the animals you see here, plus rare glimpses of the reintroduced wolves and the occasional exciting bear sighting.

Erica's Top 5: Wildlife Hotspots
3 Lake Clark
National Park in Alaska

As mentioned in my story **"Worth the Cost?" on page 131**, my Lake Clark adventure is the most expensive thing I've done to date. But if you love **bears** and have the cash to swing a visit to this remote park, do it!

Never in my wildest dreams did I think I would someday be SAFELY standing within 35 feet of **bears** in the wild – much less mothers and their cubs! I can't even put into words the magical feeling of this place. It's tough to beat seeing 20+ **bears** a day, waking up to them foraging in the field outside my room and spending hours and hours each day watching them. Photographing these amazing creatures in their habitat is an unforgettable experience.

My Lake Clark experience demonstrated a vivid example of how humans impact the lives and behavior of wild animals. The **bears** here have the food and habitat they need to thrive, and most importantly, they're not hunted. With no threat from man and no stress to find food, these **bears** live in harmony with the few lodges in the area.

These massive brown **bears** not being at all bothered by our presence is a sharp contrast to bears in the lower 48 who are running out of space to just be… **bears**. Visiting Lake Clark showed me that it IS possible for humans and wildlife to share our natural world.

I am so glad Alaska has so much land set aside for these and other majestic creatures to thrive. I also saw a **wolf**, some **river otters**, a **fox** and **bald eagles** during my stay. I can't wait to go back! The uncertainty of life in 2020 has only solidified my mantra of "someday is code for never." I'd been saying "someday" about a photographic **bear** adventure for almost eight years! I'm so glad I went before it became an unattainable dream. The memories will be with me forever, and that's well worth the cost.

In truth, all of Alaska is amazing and full of wildlife thriving alongside mankind. Every nook, cranny and town is worth exploring. Get off the cruise ship, find the road less traveled and go see what you can find!

Lake Clark is such an amazing reserve for Alaskan Brown Bears. Mama bears and cubs roam beaches and fields of grass next to forests with no fear of being hunted by the humans visiting the few lodges in the area. In fact, the only aggressor in the area are the male bears.

I captured images of the fox and otter we spotted, but most of the time I was blissfully clicking away at the bears. I even took breaks! One large bear put on a fun show scratching his back on a tree nearby... right when I was taking one of my shooting breaks. I just enjoyed the show!

Erica's Top 5: Wildlife Hotspots

4 Chobe
National Park in Botswana, Africa

This park is high on my "Gotta go back!" list. I visited back in 2008 on a trip with my sister, and I only had a Nikon D2X at the time. That camera had only 12 megapixels!!! For comparison, my current cameras have 36 and 45.7 MP. Big difference!

Sub-par gear aside, it was still an amazing trip. Even though I didn't do any photography-specific tours, I saw more wildlife than I ever could have hoped for on our one-day trip to Chobe. Yep, you read that right, one day only! It was a side trip excursion from our stay in the Victoria Falls area across the border in Zambia. I wish I'd had a week.

It was so exciting to go for a ride in the Africa bush and see **zebras** and **giraffes** in their natural habitat! We saw more **elephants** than I could count, and watching them play in the water was pure joy. The exotic **kudu** and **impala** are just beautiful. Seeing these amazing creatures in their natural habitat and not confined in a zoo setting was wonderful. The only thing I didn't see were any predators. I sooooo wish I'd had more time to explore this park!

If photography is your goal, I recommend going on a specific photography tour that lets you catch sunrise and sunset lighting. And this is one of those places where I emphatically say DON'T WAIT! Human encroachment on habitat is an ongoing global issue that is forever changing the landscape and wildlife around us. It's easy to think these places will always be there, but many are endangered and numerous animals are threatened with extinction.

This is one place I am determined to return to for more exploration, hopefully sooner rather than later! (Just so long as it's not "someday!")

Chobe is a playground for all sorts of cool looking animals! I've never seen such an array of wildlife in any single park.

Above is a handsome kudu, with an elegant impala to the right. Zebras are to the right (yes, that is a zebra butt). The striped lady is quite pregnant! The oasis below was a haven for elephants, and they truly take the "playground" concept to heart when they cool off by splashing around in the water.

Below is a monitor lizard I spotted, and the opposite page has giraffes (...see the bird on the top one's neck? I caught that later!) and just one of the colorful birds, a lilac-breasted roller, that was in reach of my lens. And this is only a sampling! Chobe is an African paradise, and I can't wait to go back.

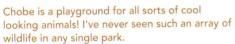

Erica's Top 5: Wildlife Hotspots

5 Grand Teton
National Park in Wyoming

Grand Teton National Park is the sister park of Yellowstone that, somehow, most people don't even know exists! In fact, I had been to Yellowstone five times before I ventured further south in the Rocky Mountains and discovered what I'd been missing.

Her smaller size by no means diminishes her beauty; in fact, she more than makes up for it with flashy mountain peaks and some of the world's best sunrises. But I'm not here to talk about the awesome landscapes! This section is for wildlife, and the Tetons has more than enough of her share.

First you can get up close and personal with a busy **beaver** while capturing sunrise at Schwabachers Landing **(see "Take the Risk, or Not?" on page 96)**. You're likely to see **fox, bighorns, bison and more**. You might even spot a **moose** or two! In the winter months, thousands of **elk** apparently peruse the lowlands – I've yet to capture that, but it's on my list. I've never witnessed that many elk in one place. You can apparently even take a sleigh ride out into the herd!

The Tetons has all the animals you're likely to see in Yellowstone, just compacted into a smaller area. Don't get me wrong – there's still plenty of outdoors to roam and tourists still love it! There has been many a traffic jam in spring when the **bears** come out of hibernation and you can get lucky enough to see the playful cubs. Still, the Tetons never feel as crowded as Yellowstone.

The park is located next to Jackson Hole, so lodging can be pricey. There are ways to visit on a budget, however! If you're not up for camping, I like to stay at Colter Bay Cabins, which are adorably rustic with an old-park feel; they are also close to many of the park highlights. A new favorite is The Hatchet Inn, just outside the park and close to Oxbow Bend, one of my favorite sunrise spots. **(See Fav Locations, page 188.)**

Again, early spring and fall are best for viewing wildlife due to the cooler weather. If you visit in winter, research which roads are open, as mountain parks have limited access to treacherous areas.

The Tetons never disappoint in the wildlife department! Some of my absolutely favorite bear images have been captured there – see "A Gloomy and Grizzly Experience" on page 42, and "Bear-ly Holding On" on page 108.

I've also seen pelicans, owls, and even a marmot up a fallen tree (pic on left page)! Plus moose, osprey, bighorn sheep, bison, beavers, more bears... did I mention bears???

The Tetons are a must-see for any wildlife enthusiast.

TOP 5 FAV LOCATIONS

Erica's Top 5: Favorite Locations
1. Bow Lake
Banff National Park in Alberta, Canada

If you were to ask me where I'd want to be this instant, it would be breathing in the crisp mountain air at **Bow Lake** off the Icefields Parkway in Banff National Park. With **Crow Foot Mountain** rising up majestically from the shores and a massive, powerful waterfall below **Bow Glacier** just a few miles up stream, the beauty of this area brings my spirit and soul peace and happiness.

Where to stay:

If that's not enough to entice you, add in one of the coolest places you can stay and you have almost pure harmony in my opinion. The **Num-Ti-Jah Lodge** started as a hunting "shack" and evolved to a 16 room lodge by 1960; it still runs on it's own generators and has much of the original log and stone architecture. The rooms are charming and the in-house restaurant serves amazing meals in their dining room each night.

There is a campground nearby if you're on a budget, but I personally love being able to wake up, pull on a hat, and step out to heaven just a few steps away. I've had the joy of staying here twice over the past five years, and can't wait to visit again.

The Num-Ti-Jah Lodge is on the north side of Bow Lake, with trails in the area to sights such as the impressive Bow Glacier Falls.

More to do:

The lake and lodge are nestled along one of the most amazing stretches of scenic roadway, the **Icefields Parkway**. This roadway is full of all my favorite things: glaciers, hiking, wildlife, mountains, cascades and glacier-fed lakes. Just typing this sentence is making me sigh with happiness as I recall my wonderful adventures in the area!

A few trails leave right from Bow Lake, but there are more sights just a little ways up the road, all within a 30-minute drive. **Peyto Lake** is less than 5 miles up the road, and the short uphill hike to the overlook is well worth the climb (bring cleats in winter). **Mistaya Canyon**, just 20 miles further, is one of the most beautiful displays of the carving power of water, and also well worth the climb back up to the parking area. The last spot is an overlook with a short walk, **Howse Pass Overlook**, just a few miles past Mistaya before you reach the intersection with David Thompson Highway, known as The Crossing.

There's even more to see in every direction from Bow Lake, but these few sites will keep you busy for a while. If you head to the Canadian Rockies, I recommend taking as much time to explore as you can!

Peyto Lake, above, is just one of the beautiful sights that's a short drive away from Bow Lake, below, on the Icefields Parkway, right. The area is stunning in summer and fall, from lush green fields to dustings of early winter snow.

You can even get snow in July! Best option for a vehicle on the Icefields Parkway is AWD or 4WD.

Erica's Top 5: Favorite Locations

Lamar Valley (in winter)
Yellowstone National Park in Wyoming

I have mentioned **Yellowstone** quite a bit in this book and have even shared a winter tale or two, but it's just so amazing in winter that it deserves to be mentioned again, and again, and again… Heck, everyone has heard of Yellowstone! It's so popular that the park can feel crowded during tourist season. If you're like me and are NOT a fan of big crowds, and if you're willing to venture out in winter, you'll discover that Yellowstone is pure magic when it's filled with puffy white snow that starkly highlights animal tracks.

Where to stay:

The interior of the park is closed to the everyday visitor in the winter (you can visit with reservations on a snowcoach), but the **Northern Road** route is open year round for travelers! This can take you from Gardiner to Cooke City, Montana, with access to **Mammoth Hot Springs** and **Lamar Valley**. If you want to venture farther into the park, you'll need to look into the park's winter tours and rentals. They're pricey but a whole lot of fun!

You can stay at Mammoth and other places inside the park, but I found my favorite place just outside the park in **Gardiner, Montana, at the Super 8**! Not only do I get a free hot breakfast in the morning, but the hotel was recently remodeled and everything is nice, comfy and clean. It's about a 15-minute drive into the park, but there's plenty of wildlife to see along the way. I also enjoy having a grocery store right across the street, and you won't find a better meal than at the **Cowboy's Lodge and Grill** – the chili is a welcome treat after being out in the elements on a -20 degree (Fahrenheit) morning!

More to do:

I never tire of seeing bison with snow clinging to their fluff and ice dripping from their chins. A winter bonus for photographers is that wildlife is easier to spot in contrast to the snow! I've seen **elk, bison, foxes, coyotes and wolves** on almost every trip. The northern part of Yellowstone in winter will keep you plenty busy with snow-dusted wildlife and stunning frosty panoramas, but don't forget to walk the **boardwalks around Mammoth Hot Springs** as well.

Be aware that the weather in this part of the country is unpredictable in winter, so it's safest to travel in an AWD or 4WD vehicle, even on the plowed roads. Plan each outing as though you might get stuck in the snow. Have your vehicle filled with blankets, snacks, water and such. Help can often be a ways away, so it's best to be prepared for any eventuality. Yellowstone in winter is worth the risk - just take care to be safe!

Yellowstone in winter is a whole new experience. Blankets of snow lie undisturbed except for the prints of animals, from bison trails laying furrows through the blank canvas, to paw prints and divots from foxes diving for mice.

Though the park's popular areas around Old Faithful are closed to general travelers in winter, there is still plenty to see in the northern part of Yellowstone. You'll find hot springs with billowing steam made more evident in the crisp winter air, and stunning sunrise colors glowing against the stark landscape.

Even with the unpredictable weather, Yellowstone in winter is definitely worth the adventure!

The vistas and drives in Custer State Park are a stunning surprise to those who visit the Black Hills just to see Mount Rushmore. Bikers are no strangers to the unique beauty of the Black Hills and come to ride here any time the weather is nice, from the Sturgis Rally in the summer to the cooler weather in the fall.

Erica's Top 5: Favorite Locations

3 Little Devils Tower
Custer State Park in South Dakota

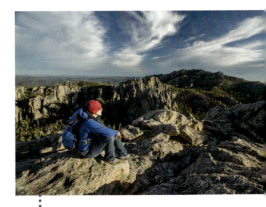

I'm fortunate to live at the base of the beautiful **Black Hills of South Dakota**, so it is only appropriate that one of my favorite locations is right here at home. And it's very specific, as it's my absolute favorite hike in the area: **Little Devils Tower**. You have a couple of options where to start: you can park at the trailhead area to start the gradual uphill climb of 1.5 miles, or if that's full you can park on the back side of nearby **Sylvan Lake** and take the half-mile trail that connects to the trailhead. Many people hike the popular Trail 9 to **Black Elk Peak** for the panoramic views, but I prefer Little Devils Tower's stunning views of both Black Elk Peak and the iconic **Cathedral Spires**. The hike is a lovely climb through the ponderosa pines, with an adventurous climb through boulders at the top (you can skip this part if you're not up for a bit of climbing). The trail is also a nice length for sunrise and sunset treks, so you don't have to get up too ridiculously early (mornings are NOT my friend) or hike too terribly far in the dark.

Where to stay:

As a local I get to take off to Custer State Park from the comfort of my own home, but I've checked out some of the park's accommodations on stay-cations or other occasions. I highly recommend staying in any of the historic lodges in the park, such as the recently remodeled, though still charmingly rustic, **State Game Lodge** in the middle of the park, known for hosting Presidents Coolidge and Eisenhower. Near the trailhead is **Sylvan Lake Lodge** (pictured to the right), and there's a broad selection of other **lodges and cabins** throughout the park.

More to do:

The Little Devils Tower hike (not to be confused with Devils Tower Monument over the border in Wyoming) may only keep you busy for part of a day, but everything the park and the whole area have to offer could keep you busy for weeks! There are a ton of hikes all around the area, including a fun one-mile loop around **Sylvan Lake**. Be sure to plan enough time to enjoy drives through the park, including the road that the trailhead is on, **Needles Highway**. I also recommend the **Wildlife Loop** that circles the southern part of the park, and the truly unique **Iron Mountain Road** with pigtail bridges and tunnels framing **Mount Rushmore National Memorial**. (See the **story on page 142,** where I sat on top of one of the tunnels!)

There are a ton of sights to see outside of the park. You can make a full day of visiting Mount Rushmore, along with nearby **Wind Cave National Park** and the private mountain carving **Crazy Horse** just outside the town of Custer. You could spend a whole week in just the southern Black Hills and still not see everything! For example, a fantastic side trip from Custer is **Jewel Cave National Monument**, well worth the 30 minute drive. It's the largest cave in the Black Hills and the 4th longest in the world, and still being explored!

These are just a few highlights. The whole area is filled with so many amazing sights that it seems a bit silly for me to single out just one trail, but hey, it's my favorite. I love how a vista point reminds me of what is important in life. Standing high atop the world and seeing the vastness of the planet is always awe-inspiring to me, reminding me of how truly small I am in this huge place we call Earth.

It's always fun to see my progress over the years! The image below was shot in 2004, while the image at the right is from my 2018 Tetons adventure.

Erica's Top 5: Favorite Locations
4 Oxbow Bend
Grand Teton National Park in Wyoming

If you've been through the book already, you've probably figured out that Grand Teton National Park is one of my favorite places to go. Being just a day's drive away from the Black Hills makes it an easy getaway for me; couple that with awesome landscapes and wildlife galore, and you've got a photographer's paradise!

Narrowing it down to a more specific location is tough, but I'd have to go with **Oxbow Bend**, a large river bend in the middle of the eastern side of the park. Oxbow Bend was one of the first places to amaze and stick with me from my early photography years. When my mom and I made a trip to the Tetons in 2004, I knew I was experiencing a magical place. One of my favorite images from that trip is of Oxbow Bend, and on slide film no less! Since then, I have to photograph this spot on every trip I take to the Tetons, even though it's frequently packed with tourists and there's a million images already out there. It still looks different and stunning to me every time, and it's always worth the shot.

Where to stay:

I've stayed all over the park, but my new favorite place is the **Hatchet Resort** just outside of the park with - you guessed it - easy access to Oxbow Bend. I usually head into the park on the east side from Rapid City on Highway 287, so it's a great place for me to set up base. You can also check out the **Colter Bay Cabins** or **Jackson Lake Lodge**. All three places are set up like motels where you can park your car right by the entrance to your room, which is great for easily bringing your gear and luggage in at night.

More to do:

I enjoy all of the wonderful areas around Oxbow Bend as well, from looking for **bears** along **Pilgrim Creek** to looking for **moose** and **elk** amongst the willows near **Jackson Lake Lodge**. Plus, some of the tastiest and best priced food in the park is just down the road at **Signal Mountain Lodge**. They even cater to the gluten-free, like me! Not gonna lie, I basically eat lunch there EVERY DAY!

There's even more to do on the many roads in and out of the park. Animals and beautiful light abound in the Tetons area, so be sure to explore! In mountain areas its always a good idea to travel in AWD or 4WD vehicles, and pack plenty of food and water if you'll be away from civilization.

Oxbow Bend never disappoints, with the large bend presenting so much water to reflect the mountains and sky that it looks more like a lake in photographs. It's the perfect canvas for sunrise and sunset compositions – some of the most stunning colors I've seen in the sky are in the Tetons.

Oxbow Bend is also a great launching point for some of the best scenery in the area. The mountains are an iconic backdrop for landscapes, and the area is a haven for wildlife.

No other mountain lake area I've visited has quite the amazing blend of scenery as Swift Current Lake. From sage grass and wildflowers to puffy clouds in clear blue skies, this secluded spot has all the best that Glacier has to offer.

Swift Current isn't the only lake to provide gorgeous scenery in this area! There are other beautiful lakes you can hike to, such as Grinnell Lake on the trek up to Grinnell Glacier, as seen to the right with bright wildflowers adding pops of color to the scene.

Erica's Top 5: Favorite Locations

5 Swift Current Lake
Glacier National Park in Wyoming

My final featured favorite place is one that I wish I could visit more often, but a long 12-hour drive to **Swift Current Lake in Glacier National Park** makes it a rare treat. In truth, I've only ever stayed in this area twice, in 2007 and 2015. Even with only two visits under my belt, my heart yearns to see this lake and its mountains again. Glacier is a wilder park than most in the US, and Swift Current is in an area that's more remote than most. A 12-mile road branches off the highway and ends at this pristine lake, where you'll find a beautiful lodge and some of the United States' best hiking trails.

Where to stay:

Since this location is remote, you've got to plan ahead if you want to secure a room at one of the two places to stay, or the sole campground. Most will want to stay at the **Many Glacier Hotel** (pictured below), as it's full of historic character and charm, and you can simply step out the lobby door to find yourself on the lake shore. The down side to this accommodation is that you'll have to haul your luggage and gear a long way to get to any room! I suggest staying at the **Swiftcurrent Motor Inn** so you can park by your room and easily get your stuff in and out of your vehicle. The lake shore is just a minute's drive away, or you can just take a nice walk to get there!

More to do:

Though more planning is needed for accommodations at this location, it's well worth the effort. Numerous amazing sights and trails are just outside your door, and Swiftcurrent is one of the **most serene lakes** you can find. Simply wake up to **watch the sunrise** and then **head down a trail**! Parking is limited here, so staying at the lake instead of limiting yourself to a day trip removes stress and lets you enjoy the lake more. A word to the wise though – there are **bears** in this section of the park (a bit more dangerous than the beautiful **bear grass**, pictured below), so listen to the rangers, do some research and be prepared.

Proud Member of PPA — Professional Photographers of America

Erica's Top 5: Bonus Tip

Join An Organization

You may be surprised that I, someone who gets insanely nervous in crowds and when meeting new people, would encourage you to go out and join an organization, of all things! But I've been involved in many groups and clubs over the years, and I've always learned from the experiences. Sure, there are numerous places online where you can learn new techniques, or sites where you can pay for a photographer's best business tips... but can you ask a video questions? Will a video help you cover a wedding if you're too sick to shoot? That's a definite NO. **I've learned that human interaction is an important part of growing as an artist.**

Shall I start at the beginning? Well, not the full beginning since I can't mention every group I've been involved in, and I mainly want to discuss **the organization that's been the most beneficial for my photography: Professional Photographers of America.**

It was only five years ago that I joined PPA, and it was mainly for the free camera equipment insurance! I hadn't even heard of the organization until I was researching coverage after a very stressful "What the f?" moment where I nearly killed my camera. **(See story on page 52.)**

After being an inactive member for a year, I saw they had a competition I could enter as a member, the PPA International Photographic Competition. I submitted images and earned three merits, whatever those were. I didn't realize this was quite an accomplishment until I met fellow photographer and PPA member Johnny Sundby. He explained the significance of merits (it's how you earn PPA Degrees) and noted that it usually takes new members a while just to earn their first merit. I have to admit, it changed my perspective and I got excited about more than just the PPA insurance!

With this and other discussions, Johnny became a mentor of sorts and helped me see what PPA is really all about. We even went to **Imaging USA** that first year, PPA's annual photo convention. It's quite an event, lasting several days with 80+ speakers, over 500 vendors and upwards of 10,000 photographers in attendance. I was nervous about all the social gatherings, like classes and awards ceremonies, so I talked Toni into tagging along as a guest. What can I say? Talking to new people is scary! But happily, I fell in love with all of the inspiration I came home with, and I even made some new friends.

Later on that year Johnny advised me to also join the local affiliate PPA groups, and I'm now a member in both Wyoming and South Dakota. First and foremost, one of the

Above is one of my latest digitally hand painted images, my imagining of a Sahara carpool, ha! PPA has encouraged me to reach new heights in my photography.

My involvement in PPA has brought me to new heights, such as excelling at this new (to me) art form, and earning awards and accolades I may have never thought possible, like joining PPA's Team USA, chosen out of thousands of photographers worldwide!

Photo © Alex Arnett

best things that came out of joining an organization was the friendships I made. Having this support system around me has lifted me up higher as an artist than I feel would have been possible on my own. Often times we settle for "good enough," or are so involved with our work that we don't see the flaws. Having people around you who will provide **honest, constructive feedback pushes you to be better**, and can even set you on a path you may have never considered!

Just last year I had an image for competition that I wanted to have a "painted" look, and not knowing how to digitally paint something, I used a filter effect. I thought it looked great and was in love with the image! But when shared with a PPA friend, the first words out of her mouth were, "Did you use a filter?" It hurt that my work seemed sub-par, not gonna lie… but it hit home. I could do better! Next thing I knew, I'd dusted off the digital pen tablet I had shoved aside after I didn't excel at using it right away (hey, we all love instant gratification), and I put in the time and practice it takes to improve at doing something difficult.

Since that push outside my comfort zone, I've gone on to paint many whimsical scenes and beloved pet portraits for clients. It's a great skill to have in the off-season, and it's an amazing creative outlet. Even though I still consider myself primarily a landscape and nature photographer, joining PPA has taught me that I don't need to box myself in to just one genre. **I can be anything I want to be!**

If you look under my name on **page 151** and Johnny's **on page 13**, you'll see "M. Photog. Cr., CPP" – these represent degrees, or ranks, bestowed upon members as they earn merits through efforts such as excelling in PPA print competitions, or by contributing to the photographic community through educational efforts. The purpose of the degrees are to **challenge oneself**, and it pushes us to not only continually improve our work but to also **help elevate the photography field as a whole**. Earning the status of Master Photographer and getting involved with helping others who are passionate about photography has been a wonderful experience for me. It has helped build my confidence!

Being involved with an organization like PPA also helps photographers **stay up-to date on new technology and provides a network of support for their business.** Plus, **seeing each other's work can inspire new ideas!** In fact, as I write this piece I am also watching the live judging of PPA's International Photographic Competition. I'm getting inspired while I wait for my images to be judged by some of the finest photographers in the nation. (Ha, it's a bit stressful too!) I am still pushing for more, now working on my Master Artist degree so I can improve not only my technical photography skills, but also my Photoshop® skills.

In short, get out there and find your PPA! **Find the organization that fits you**, one where you're involved with actual people. These in-person educational opportunities will not only **build up your photographic skills**, but will provide you with **inspiration and drive**. And even better are the **friendships that are worth their weight in gold.**

MAKE
EVERY
DAY
AN
adventure

FINAL WORD
how the f did this happen?

by Antonia Kucera

Best Friends and Travel Buddies, Decades in the Making

When you meet Erica, she tends to leave an impression. I'm often forgetful about these things, often not remembering who I might've gone to a movie with long ago and usually having to stop and count the years on my birthday to remember how old I am! (Don't ask, I actually prefer to stop counting…) But my goofy memory can be stellar when something is unusual enough to get stuck there. And that's why I remember meeting Erica.

It was my senior year of high school, and I was lucky enough to get selected as one of the art and photography students who would go on a weekend road trip to Yellowstone. Though the famous national park was just a day's travel away, I'd never been there! I don't remember much about the drive over, other than the other vanload of students got a flat tire (nobody got hurt, thankfully), and I snoozed at some point and woke up to majestic views in the Bighorn Mountains. I remember the excitement of finally getting to Yellowstone itself, marvelling at the billowing geyser steam as we pulled into Mammoth Hot Springs, where we'd be split up into cabins for our stay.

Heck, I don't even remember the name of the gal I was roomed with! We got along well, I remember, even though I was the quiet and shy type. We'd just finished settling in when a classmate ran up and said, "Hey, we're all heading to the cabin down the way, some chick's got FOOD!"

Well, enough said. I hadn't thought to bring food, much less a camping grill, which is exactly where I met Erica for the first time – she was perched behind a propane grill on a cabin porch in Yellowstone. This is quite the perfect picture of her: as you should know by now, she's all about nature and cool gear! (To clarify, I'm sure the teachers had meal plans for us, I just don't remember… camp-style grilled food is ALWAYS better anyway!)

As much as Erica is the type to leave an impression, I'm more the type to fly under the radar at first. We weren't immediate besties or anything, but we hung out at times that

year, and off and on throughout our college years (she was back and forth from California, I went to study photography and got into graphic design at Black Hills State University, near home). After Erica gravitated back to the Black Hills post-college, however, life pulled us closer and closer, until we reached that point in a friendship where one knows what the other is thinking. More and more, Erica was the friend I was excited to talk with about everything going on in life, and the friend I was so excited and proud to see succeed at what she took on in life. (Still proud. Awww, I'm getting sappy!)

So of course, Erica was the first person I was excited to talk to about the Banff Film Festival after another friend had taken me to enjoy the experience at a local theater. (Thank you Terri!!!) I'd been slack-jawed at the amazing cinematography and the stunning vistas. I'd never heard of Banff National Park – in fact had NO IDEA there were these big, beautiful parks further north of Yellowstone in Canada!

After my first round of jaw-dropping films, I immediately called Erica. I let out a big sigh and said, "I wanna go to Banff!" Of course, if you know Erica, you know she started planning a trip right away. So just one year later in 2014, we went on our first big adventure together (see story on page 46). Ha, I just wanted her to go to the film festival with me, but in true Erica fashion, she introduced me to the real thing.

I fell in love with the Canadian Rockies, and Erica's love for travel rubbed off on me. After that we managed to go on at least one fun trip every year, except for when my pesky health issues got in the way (see story on page 76), and up until good 'ol 2020 came along and put a halt to joyful travel.

I try to find silver linings, though, and the one we found in 2020 was that we got to finish this book! As happened to many in 2020, my time became available after the pandemic led to the loss of my job. I'd built up a hodgepodge assortment of skills while working in advertising for 20 years, and thankfully many of them formed the rudiments of what I'd need to design a book. Erica has been the type of friend who has been there through thick and thin, from the fun adventures and girl-time hangouts, to the terrible times of ambulance rides and canceled plans. So when she brought up the idea of making a book, I was happy to be able to say "I can do that!" and have the opportunity to give back to my best friend.

And so we have this beautiful, shining silver lining to the trying year of 2020. The knocks keep coming this year, but I'm holding on. This too, shall pass, as the saying goes… and as Erica and I say, we WILL travel again. Adventure awaits.

Antonia Kuzm

thank you
with gratitude to our Kickstarter Backers & Other Supporters

Our friends and family made this beautiful book a reality!

First off, I want to thank each and every one who supported me on Kickstarter, and in person during the fundraising campaign. Self-publishing a book is no small feat, let alone during a pandemic, so to have all of you believe in my crazy idea during these even crazier times is the most amazing thing an artist could ask for!

I have had dreams of publishing a book of my work since college, and it feels so surreal now to finally see one of my dreams come to fruition. The dream would have simply remained that – a dream – but instead, you guys all rallied behind me and helped me achieve things I could not have done on my own! So with that, Toni and I both thank you from the bottom of our hearts. Know that, at least for me, this is one of the proudest moments in my life.

Second, thank you to all of my friends and followers for sharing my posts and helping me get the word out to the public about our project. You can see what a difference it made: WE'RE PUBLISHED!

Third, I also want to thank Toni. I know working on this project was a huge undertaking with all that has been going on in her life. I am so thankful I will be able to hold this book and think of all of the adventures we have been on together. I will never forget all the laughs I had getting to create a book with my best friend, and I can't wait for our next adventure!

Lastly, I want to thank my husband. Photography may not be his thing, but he knows it means the world to me, as does going on adventures. Thank you for allowing me to be me and for not hindering my adventurous soul. I know you are not with me on all my crazy trips, but know you are always in my heart and that I always look forward to returning to your handsome smile and jokes. It is so hard to believe we have been together for 12 years, but I have to say emphatically: they have been the best years of my life. I am excited to see what the future holds, and I am thankful I have you to share it with.

It was TOUGH to sort that Kickstarter list! So... we kinda had to wing it.

Names are mostly listed in alphabetical order by first name of the primary backer. If you don't find it there, try the family name or the significant other's name. If we somehow misspelled your name, please don't hate us! We're a photographer and a designer who only use spreadsheets when we absolutely have to!

ADILFA FORD • AILEEN HARDING • AJ HOAR • AL MURCHISON • ALAN & JAMIE DUBBELDE • ALBERT DOMINGUEZ • ALEC & JODY DEMOISE • ALISON J. SCOTT • ALYSSA L. TANNER • ALYSSA & MATT SHEESLEY • AMANDA BUFFO & FAMILY • AMANDA KOZLOWSKI & FAMILY • AMANDA MCCLURE • AMANDA SCOTT • AMBER PONTIUS • ANDREA BRADY • ANDREA FORSLUND • ANDREA UNKEL • ANDREW & DIANE KNUTSON • ANDY JACKSON • ANDY OGAN • ANGELA LAWSON • ANGUS GIBBINS • ANN EADS • ANN MORROW • ANNA & URIEL GUTIERREZ • ANNE HERB • ANNE MYHRE & FAMILY • APRIL HIX • APRIL OEDEKOVEN • ARDEN NELSON • ARLANDRIA RAE BESHARA • AUDREY BELITZ • BARRY CASTETTER • BECKI TAYLOR • BECKY CRAGO • BELVA & SCOTT SIPHERD • BETTY ABELMAN • BILL BLAKE • BOB & MARY WILLS • BOB AINSWORTH • BOB WHITE • BRAD HALL • BRANDI TUINSTRA • BRANDON KEYSER & FAMILY • BROOKE COSHOW • BRYAN PERKINS • CALVIE ELLIS • CANDACE YVETTE TKACHUCK • CANDENCE ALEXANDER & FAMILY • CANDYCE HERMAN • CAROL & PAT SHANAHAN • CAROL DAVIES • CAROL VALENTINE • CAROLINE STANLEY • CAROLYN DELORME • CHAD WAGNER • CHANCE B. WHELCHEL & MICHAEL S. STANLEY • CHARLES LEHMANN & RUBY • CHERI DE LONG • CHERYL SCHMIDT • CHRIS & MISSY JOHNSON • CHRIS VANDER VELDE • CHRIS WOOLEY • CHRIS YUSHTA • CHRISTINA MYERS • CHRISTINE & DON BACKENS • CHRISTY DERYNCK • CHUCK ANDERSON • CLAY DILLON • COLLEEN THORSON-SCHWEIGER & TODD SCHWEIGER • COLTON PRYOR • CONNIE HUBBARD • CONNIE STANLEY • CORRIE PFEIFLE • CRAIG MOUNT • CRAIG STEINLEY • CRYSTAL TREVINO • CYNDE LANDRITH • CYNDIE HAMILTON • DALE HOUSEHOLDER • DAN & BARBARA WENK • DAN RAY • DANA ROSE • DARLA DREW • DAVID ENRIQUEZ • DAVID HORAN • DAVID, MEGAN, & AVERY VETCH • DEB HAYES ZIMMERMAN • DELLA WATTERS • DENIS PAYNE • DENNIS POPP • DIANE FITCH • DIANE STAEFFLER • DONNA HOFELDT • DORIS DORGAN • DOUG & MARGE MORTON • DR. DANIEL & NICOLE LOCHMANN • DUSTIN HOFFMAN • EGIJA HARTMANE-SALEM • ELAINE & RICHARD KARSKY • ELIZABETH WOOD • EMILY MATTER • ERIC LEE • ERIC STAHL • ERIN HOLMES • ERIN HOPE & FAMILY • EVA & STEVE BAREIS • FRANK LEE RUGGLES • GELEA ICE • GLEN HAGEN • HEATHER VANDERPOOL • HOPE CANADAY • ISABELLA YELLOWTAIL • JACKIE SMITH • JACLYN KENNISON • JACOB A. THOMPSON • JACQUELINE MARIE RYAN • JACQUELINE WORTH • JAMEE ALLGIER • JAN HINES • JANET GREER • JANNA HOPE • JASON & BRIDGET HERMANSON • JASON SCHAEFER • JEAN MCLAURY • JEANNE WAGNER & FAMILY • JEFF & PAM VANCUREN • JEFF MENKENS • JENN GOAD & FAMILY • JENNI KNEZOVICH • JENNIFER LEMAY • JENNIFER MEIER • JENNIFER SCHROEDER & FAMILY • JEREMY & EMILY LICHTY • JEREMY RYLE • JEREMY WALLA • JERRY ARDENSE • JESSICA SEVER • JIM & CAROLYNE STAVANGER • JIM CUNNINGHAM • JIM HARVEY • JIM JEFFRIES • JIM KENDALL • JIM PLUMMER • JODIE LEMKE • JOE & JANINE BELEY • JOHN & CAROLYN TEIGEN • JOHN DWYER • JOHN HUDSON • JOHNNY & STEPH SUNDBY • JOLENE GEARY • JOSH KATZ • JUDITH SAWYER • JUDY & CRAIG HODSON • JUDY REINFORD • JULAINE JAGER • JULIE & JEREMY TONAR • JULIE MECHALEY • JULIE PRAIRIE • JUNIOR WAGNER • KADIE & TYLER PAWICH • KANDACE KREUN • KARA MILLS • KAREN BIELMAIER • KAREN MAHONEY • KAREN MCCALL • KAREN MONTIEL • KARISA SIEVERDING • KATE GALLUP & FAMILY • KATH & JIM WHITE • KATHI BUESCHER • KAYE & JOHN DUFFIELD • KELLY HARNETT • KELLY WHITAKER • KENDRA PERRY-KOSKI • KENNY PUTNAM • KERRI BROOKS • KEVIN EILBECK • KIM & JAKE KUCERA • KIMBERLY PEZESHKI • KORI & JERRY BERTINO • KORY BUMGARDNER • KRISTAL KRAFT • KRISTIN NEUHARDT • KRISTIN WHITE • KRISTY STEEVES • KRYSTAL JONES • LARRY LARSON • LAURA & DUSTIN FLOYD • LAURA GIBSON • LESLIE & LARRY JACKSON • LESLIE BOHLE • LESLIE KITTEN • LESLIE PREBLE & FAMILY • LINDA HAGEN • LINDSAY K. GRONOS • LISA & BARRY ACKLY • LISA ASP • LISA CASE • LISA LOEZEL • LIZ HARVEY • LIZ LEYVA • LOUISE HARVEY • LYNN BROWER • MAMIE STEWART YELLOWTAIL • MARCIA VANBACH • MARGARET J DORGAN • MARIE MARTINEAU SANDBERG • MARK A. NILSEN • MARK GARDNER • MARKUS ERK & CANDY ERK MANTHEY • MARNI CHRISTENSEN • MARY BETH & CHARLIE JOHNSON • MATT ONEILL • MEG WARDER • MEGAN CHRISTOPHER • MELANIE WILKE • MELINDA BOYD • MELINDA HARRIS • MELISSA MOSS • MELISSA THOMPSON • MICHAEL MOWBRAY • MICHAEL WARD • MICHELLE CONNOR • MICHELLE HAGEN • MICHELLE LOFFELMACHER • MIKE & CRISTINA KOPREN • MIKE & JULIA SISSON • MIKE MAGDA • MIKE STE MARIE • MONTY MCNABB • MYRA LOOMER • NANCY ASHLEY • NANCY STATZ • NICCI BLAKEMAN • NICHOLAS ANGELIDES • NICK & LORRI ROMBOUGH • NICOLE GIVENS • PATRICIA AITKEN • PATRICK J. O'LEARY • PAUL & MONEIK STEPHENS • PAUL & SANDY PFEIFER • PAUL HORSTED • PAUL JENSEN • PEGGY COLE • PET WELLER • PHYLLIS MARTENS • PHYLLIS SCHULTZ • PORTIA SHAO • RACHEL NELSON • REBECCA DEWITT • REBECCA FUGATE • REBECCA NELSON • REBECCA & CLINT PICKREL • REGINA RANGEL-SANCHEZ • RHONDA DESCHAMP • RICHARD & JOYCE KUCERA • RICK MILLS • RICK MONHEIM • RJ PIEPER • RO & DUFF MCCAFFERTY • ROBIN CUMMINS • ROD & GOGIE ENSTAD • ROGER & GAYEDENE (†) JINDRA • ROSEMARY HARVEY • RUSSELL & PAULA JENSEN • RUTH MCINNIS • SCOTT HOFFMAN • SHAINA HARGENS • SHANNON BRINKER • SHARON CHONTOS • SHEILA JOHNSON • SHEILA KELLY • SHERRY L. VIALL • SHIRLEY MCPHEETERS • STACIA SHAPAN • STACIE BAKER • STAN ROBERTSON & FAMILY • STEPHANIE HJELMFELT • STEVE GULLIKSON • STEWART MOEN • SUZY ADAMS BARTSCHER • TAMMY BARROWS • TAMMY BLACKMER • TAMMY LARSON • TARA BURIAN • TARA MECHALEY & FAMILY • TARRAH JINDRA • TAYLOR THOMPSON • TERESA HOFER • TERRI & TJ ROSSER • TERRY & BRENDA THOMAS • TIM CAMERON • TIM SOELZER • TOM NAVAUGHTNY • TRACY MAILLOUX • VANESSA POWLES • VESTA WELLS JOHNSON • VICKY STEELMAN • WILLOW GUTIERREZ

in loving memory

Thanks for All the Cuddles, Wiggles and Giggles

One of the bitterest notes of 2020 for our little family unit is the loss of our fur baby, Peanut. Though she looked and acted like an energetic new puppy at all times, she was a little old lady in dog years. She was a special needs pup, giving us many a scare over the years when some odd little thing in her tiny body would go wonky. But she was there with cuddles any time the world got either of us down, and she always made us smile with her adorable antics.

We'll miss our Peanutter terribly, but loving this pup was worth the heartache. Rest well in puppy heaven!

With love from your humans,

Erica and Adam